Audio Made Easy

To access online media visit:
www.halleonard.com/mylibrary

Enter code:

1355–0901–2084–8041

Audio Made Easy

Audio Made Easy

Or How to Be a Sound Engineer
Without Really Trying

FIFTH EDITION

IRA WHITE

Hal Leonard Books
An Imprint of Hal Leonard LLC

Fifth edition published in 2017 by Hal Leonard Books
An Imprint of Hal Leonard LLC
7777 West Bluemound Road
Milwaukee, WI 53213

Trade Book Division Editorial Offices
33 Plymouth St., Montclair, NJ 07042

First edition published in 1997 by Hal Leonard Corporation

Printed in the United States of America

Book design by Kristina Rolander

Library of Congress Cataloging-in-Publication Data is available upon request.

ISBN 978-1-4950-7507-0

www.halleonardbooks.com

CONTENTS

7. Cause & Effect

8. Signal Corps

9. Power Tools

10. Pumping Paper

11. For the Record

12. Audio by Design

13. Packing Up

Track Listing

INTRODUCTION

NAVIGATING THE COMPLEXITIES

As far back as I can remember, people have been asking for a complete book on professional audio that they can understand. Unfortunately, most books cover only certain aspects of audio and are fraught with pages of formulas and abstract elements that tax the absorption rate of the average person in a world where most would guess that *transient response* is what you get when you ask a bum a question. Or that Hertz is just a car rental company. Not exactly.

A lot of people want to get involved in sound or recording for the fun and fulfillment of it. They're not interested in writing a doctoral thesis. They're probably not going to be asked to design and run a system for Lady Gaga. However, they would like useful information, a sense of accomplishment, and some aural excitement without too much pain (Hertz?). Beyond that, audio interests can be pursued as far as the heart desires.

So I decided to write this book, which covers a little of everything without becoming too tedious. It's based on my experiences and the many questions asked of me by colleagues and customers, and it delves a little deeper into some of the more misunderstood details of digital mixers, using EQ, speaker specifics, and recording techniques. In it, I hope to furnish real-world solutions and tips that will show results and not just raise more questions. I try to accommodate a variety of equipment budgets and provide a firm foundation on which to build audio wisdom. I wish to give you the capability to soar to new heights and achieve any lofty dream you may hold dear. And I wish to retire at age 60 with millions!

Your purchasing this book helps us both toward our goals. And we can learn some important lessons along the way. So let's enjoy the journey.

Ira White

P.S. Even if you're only interested in a particular area of audio, I encourage you to read this whole book. There are tips and information within every section and application that should be helpful to you. Besides, it isn't that long. In the time it takes to add a room to your house or take a Caribbean cruise, you could read this book and still have time for a shower.

This is a work of nonfiction. The characters, incidents, and dialogues are products of the author's imagination but are not to be construed as unreal. Any resemblance to actual events or persons, living or dead, is entirely intentional though probably grossly exaggerated.

Audio Made Easy

Sound Psyche

THE PRIDE AND THE PASSION

Music is an art, and sound engineering is an extension of that art. You should first understand that you are an integral part of the overall product—not just a button pusher, but an artist who makes spontaneous decisions based on what you hear. The song is the subject, the instruments are the paint, the tone and balance are the brush strokes, and the room (or recorder) is the canvas. Your equipment ultimately gives you the ability to create the overall picture, to skillfully mix the colors, to move yourself and others to an emotional response. And as it is with any passionate endeavor, the fact that you are working hard and starving at the same time is mostly hidden by the enjoyment of your quest.

The only problem is that you need to master the basics well enough for them to run on automatic while you dedicate your time to creating. Like riding a bike, you can concentrate on where you're going and not on how to turn the pedals. And you need to feel comfortable and confident in your capabilities, especially in one-shot live situations. Just as in scuba diving, if you panic, you drown. Don't be intimidated, and keep a cool head. Things are rarely as bad as they seem, and you'll find that peace of mind promotes good judgment and will rub off on others around you, creating a sense of security and trust. That's a positive influence on the most volatile variable of working with others—chemistry.

THE GOLDEN RULE

. . . and speaking of chemistry, I'd like to mention something about social interaction. When working with other people, the fun can quickly depart if we eccentric artists get into adversarial relationships. We often try to push our opinions on others, which only puts them on the defensive. We all need to work together, but we still need to know that we are in control of our individual responsibilities.

To maintain this balance, I try to empathize with others' views. Sometimes they're right. When they're not, politely explaining the situation in overly technical jargon that neither of us can understand may help. In either case, I'll generally make a point of periodically (and sincerely) asking how things sound to those concerned. Once their defenses are down and they feel secure in having received sufficient consideration, I can maintain reasonable control in peace. Mutual respect develops. Everybody wins.

THE BROKEN RULE

I'll be passing along ideas in this book that will establish constructive guidelines. The ironic thing is that once you've mastered them, it'll be time to throw many of them out. Rules can't teach you how to create, only how someone else created. It's up to you to blaze new paths. Once you've got a little knowledge tucked away, you'll find that common sense goes a long way toward experimentation and discovery. And once you've beaten every new idea to death, you'll invariably learn that less is more.

I never fully realized how this had applied to my engineering development until I tried learning about stage lighting. I read about focal lengths, lumens, ellipsoidals and Fresnels, Roscolux colors . . . I was so proud of my wealth of knowledge. And then I saw an Emmy award–winning lighting guy do almost everything with a few par cans and four basic colors. I should have asked him how he did it without the other junk, but he probably would have said, "Sounds like you've been reading a book."

So don't let rules hold you back. And don't overcomplicate things. Keep it simple, keep an open mind, and don't hesitate to ask questions. You can learn something from everybody, and each little tidbit can be filed away in your cerebral library of audio wisdom to be called upon for crucial decisions when you least expect it. As soon as you stop testing the limits, you will go no further. Have fun, be bold, and make more coffee.

The Source Be With You

2

IF YOU WANT SPECIFICATIONS, GET A SPEC SHEET. If you want detailed features and operation, get an owner's manual. But if you want excellent general info and brilliant tips . . . welcome to the club! Hopefully, we'll take the mysticism out of audio equipment and learn how to use this stuff, taking each in its proper order of signal flow. We begin where it all starts—at the source.

ON THE LEVEL

You will most likely be dealing with a great variety of sound-producing instruments in your audio aspirations, many of which are already electronic in nature. These include CD players, iPods and smartphones, stereo or instrument preamplifiers, keyboards, and sound modules. These can plug straight into appropriate audio equipment and transfer their sounds directly and accurately. Acoustical sounds, such as vocals and acoustic instruments, cannot. They must first be converted to electronic signals to be used, so we add an incredible variety of microphones and pickups to our list of sources to accomplish this task. Which ones to use where will be discussed shortly.

Our first concern is levels. Though all these products lack the higher voltage to drive speakers (amplifiers do that), they nonetheless have a low-level voltage that we can express in a unit of audio measure called the **decibel** (or **dB**) that will let us know how potentially loud each can be in relation to another. The dB output rating, or **gain**, will be important when integrating with other equipment. Gain can be classed in two general categories: **mic level** and **line level**.

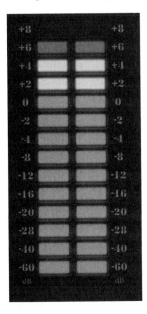

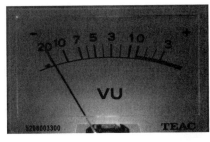

Mic level sources are the lowest and are generally associated with *passive* sources (those not driven by electrical or battery power). Microphones themselves are typically in the –60dB to –50dB range, while guitar pickups are –30dB to –20dB. *Active* (powered) line level sources like keyboards and mixers are above –20dB and can get up to a +4dB average (***unity gain***) or even higher in output. If you ever saw a VU meter on earlier analog equipment, you probably noticed that the meter read from around –20dB to +4dB (a 24dB range), and there is a big difference between the loudest and softest sounds. Now imagine adding another –40dB to the bottom range for a total of at least 64dB between the lowest and highest sources, and you can get some idea of the great variations in equipment levels. But be not dismayed, for, wonder of wonders, the mixer we use allows us to account for these differences.

MICROPHONES

Mic choice can be one of the hardest decisions because most people don't get the chance to compare many out in the real world. There are usually three or more nice choices in each class, though one will most likely have either the best sound or the best price, or both, to set it apart from the rest. Knowing which one to use takes a little bit of research. As with most products, the more you spend, the higher the quality you're more likely to get. But these days, there are some top-notch mics in almost every price range, so don't let budget kill your expectations.

When shopping for vocal handheld mics, compare through accurate speakers (preferably studio monitors) or try to get them on a trial-and-return basis to make sure they live up to your real-world expectations. Test the mic from about 3 inches. Listen for a smooth and clear sound without harshness or a shrill edge to it. One mistake novices make is to gravitate toward a mic that has the most treble and bass in its response. This can indicate undesirable peaks or a lack of midrange. The ideal mic has a natural, balanced sound as the starting point. Then you will have all the necessary sonic components to manipulate as your heart, ears, and audio system demand. Check handling noise by tapping the casings, and off-axis rejection by hearing how little it picks up when talking into the side of the mic, which can also indicate how well it rejects feedback. Finally, check industry reviews in various pro audio magazines. (I discovered some of the best-kept secrets there.) All in all, you'll discover significant differences between models.

Now, let's cover some information on microphone types.

A **dynamic** mic is a little speaker in reverse. Sound waves in the air vibrate the mic's diaphragm, moving a tiny coil back and forth around a magnet and generating a low-voltage signal. Dynamics are durable, economical, and usually have good response within 1 foot. Though they have limited sensitivity for picking up distant sources, this can be a plus in live sound, where isolation is critical. This means the mic doesn't pick up things you don't want it to.

Styles of dynamic mics include *ball mics,* with a built-in windscreen to minimize breath pop from vocals, and *pencil mics,* which are designed more as instrument mics since they don't have the windscreen. Good, affordable dynamics cost around $100 to $300. Popular standards include the Shure SM series, the Beyer M69, and the Audix OM series.

A **condenser** mic is designed with a more sensitive diaphragm for increased frequency response and distance pickup. Unlike a dynamic mic, it generates signal through a change in capacitance between two charged elements and requires a voltage source or an associated electronics pack to drive circuits in the mic. (Don't worry, I'm not sure *I* understood what

I just wrote.) The voltage needs to be supplied by an integral battery or an external source called **phantom power,** which is available on most professional mixers. (No, it's not a power boost for your system!)

Condenser styles include a variety of *pencil* (end-address) and *side-address* models, the latter being the heftier studio models with a large diaphragm that picks up from the side. Economical cardioid condensers like the Shure SM81, Audio-Technica AT4040, AKG C451, and Rode NT1000 can range from $200 to $600, while various switchable pattern and tube circuit models typically run higher, depending on how much you want to impress your "clients." (Again, check industry reviews for current "hot picks.") Less expensive battery-operated condensers can be had for under $150 and will pass in budget situations, but they lack the quality and level handling of the phantom-powered models. There are also special miniature condensers, like the Audix M1255B and the Audio-Technica AT800 series, that are designed for choirs, podiums, instruments, and other live applications.

Condensers are essential for studio recording, acoustic instrument pickup, and distance pickup, but less so for live, handheld vocals. Condensers cost more than dynamics, and their components are a bit more fragile. Personally, I find most handheld condensers have less isolation and feedback rejection than current quality dynamics like the Audix OM series, and I prefer to avoid potential noise from connection problems that can occur with 48 volts of phantom power going through a stressed mic cable.

A lesser-known design is the **ribbon** mic, currently offered by just a few manufacturers, such as Royer and Beyer. It gets its name from the very small, thin metal ribbon that serves as its element, and older designs were initially popular as those hefty desk mics on TV talk shows. Though sensitive like a condenser, most are passive (non-powered) like a dynamic and have a relatively low output level. Besides being expensive, its delicate ribbon is prone to damage. You won't see these very often, and they aren't essential in general applications, but they typically do have a unique "warm and sweet" sound.

EXPLORING THE POLES

Mics are available in a variety of pickup, or polar, patterns. **Omnidirectional** mics pick up sound in all directions, making them unsuitable in most live applications where directed pickup and feedback rejection are crucial. **Unidirectional** mics (which includes ball mics) are designed with special vents that allow sounds from the rear and sides to enter the capsule and be cancelled out. Be aware that if you try to look "cool" by wrapping your hand around the head of a ball mic, you cover up its vents and turn it into an omnidirectional, degrading its intended sound and making it more prone to feedback! The purpose of the ball is simply to house a windscreen and create some distance to the element so breath pop is diverted. The unidirectional vents are actually hidden inside.

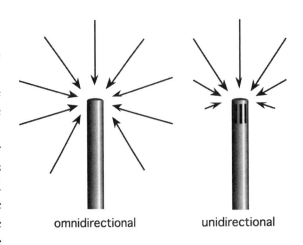

omnidirectional   unidirectional

Another unidirectional trait is **proximity effect**. If a source, such as vocal, is within 6 inches of a unidirectional mic, bass frequencies become disproportionately stronger. Some mics have a bass rolloff switch to compensate for this, or it can be controlled at the mixer by turning down the low EQ to avoid an overly "bassy" sound.

Cardioid-design unidirectionals have a medium pickup pattern, say 90° around the front of the mic, and the most rejection of sound at the rear. **Hypercardioids** are usually more expensive and have a tighter pattern of maybe 60°, making them less prone to feedback with maximum rejection to either side of the rear. **Supercardioid** is around 30° and designed more for narrow-distance pickup, many times in the form of long "shotgun" condenser mics.

Bidirectional is a lesser-used studio pattern that picks up from both front and rear, kind of like a two-sided cardioid, with greatest rejection on either side. It is only offered in special-design dynamics and in studio condensers with switchable patterns.

My pickup "degrees" are just averages because it changes depending on the frequencies. In this supercardioid mic's graphic, the blue line is the low-end pickup, the brown is the midrange, and the green is the high end. (0° is the front of the mic.) It illustrates that the overall pickup doesn't coalesce until you get into the upper ranges, so the high-frequency pattern determines the most effective pickup width.

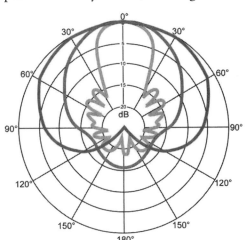

MIC TECHNIQUES

Since many of you will likely be in a less-than-ideal room environment, I will focus on close-miking techniques good for studio and live applications. With a good studio condenser, any instrument will sound natural when picked up from 3 feet away or more, but you'll also pick up bad room acoustics, noises, and any other nearby instruments with the extra level required. Close miking sounds more "in your face" and is definitely essential when isolation is important, but mic placement is critical. This is because it takes a little distance for tones from different parts of an instrument to finally mix to become its complete sound. The bigger the instrument, the greater the distance. The trick with close miking is to pick up a part of the instrument that best represents the whole thing. Subtle or subjective corrections may be accomplished through mic choice or mixer EQ.

If you choose to **stereo mic** distant sources for recording, you can use a simple "V" configuration. Place the heads *or* bases of the mics together (not touching) to form an angle of 75°–90°, each one aiming toward opposite sides of your source area. I slightly prefer the bases together because the separated elements offer a little more stereo imaging while simulating the distance between our ears, with a lot of empty space in between, a typical characteristic of sound engineers. This works well for stationary performers like choir or orchestra, but it is better to arrange the V with the mic heads together if performers will be moving around. That's because separating the mic heads would cause phase cancellations from timing anomalies between the mics as the distances of sounds they pick up change with the movement.

Now we get to the part where common sense goes a long way. *Where should the mic be placed?* Where the instrument sounds the best. *Where does the instrument sound the best?* Listen to it, Sherlock.

Acoustic Guitar

Let's start with a guy playing acoustic guitar. First, listen to the guitar from about 3–5 feet away. This natural sound will be your reference. (If it sounds like garbage, put the mic anywhere and pray.) You'll be placing the mic 6–12 inches away from the front so the picking hand won't hit it. First, pretend your ear is the mic, and listen around all the spots within 12 inches in front of the guitar. If it sounds too dull, don't

put the mic there. If it sounds too thin or hollow, ditto. When you find a spot where the guitar sounds about right, put the mic there and you're ready to roll. My usual spot is just to the side of the sound hole at the end of the fret board in front of the high-end strings. For a stereo pair, I prefer the second mic somewhere around the bridge of the guitar.

First rule: *Trust your ears.* (You didn't know you had all the answers stuck on the sides of your head, did you?) Choose a spot with the sound closest to what you're looking for. Unfortunately, this won't work if you have no clue what you want to hear. Solution: Start listening to a lot of good music and develop preferences. *Your* sound is probably written in your DNA; you just need to draw it out.

For acoustic guitar, a good condenser is preferred for stage or studio. Built-in pickups can be more convenient for live use, but most don't emulate the natural sound for critical recording in the studio. However, it can be helpful to record mic and pickup combinations to take advantage of both—the natural sound of miking and the unique tone and isolation of the pickup. If you're feeding an acoustic pickup directly through long lines, such as a snake (an extension cable of multiple mic lines), use a ***direct box***. I've also used a good wireless lapel mic in live situations with good results. Clip it on the sound hole in such a way that it doesn't sit in the hole, and EQ if needed.

Electric Guitar

With electric guitar cabinets, you have the same situation as with an acoustic instrument. Different tones come from various areas of the speaker cone, any ports or openings, and the cabinet itself. Listen close to areas of the speaker and you'll notice that the sound isn't the same from 5 feet away. A particular problem I've found is that many guitarists have their cabinets on the floor with the higher frequencies shooting under them in a narrow pattern. They adjust their tone for the very "warm" sound they're hearing while high-end "bite" is actually cranking out at speaker level—a reason many guitar rigs sound thin and edgy from a mic and audience perspective. Better that the cabinet is raised or angled up so the guitarist can hear and adjust his tone more accurately.

It's up to you to decide whether you want the close or distant sound or a combination of both, and mike accordingly. I usually mike within 6 inches at the side of the cone, pointing toward the center, and control the "edgy" treble by cutting back on the mixer high EQ. This brings out more of the guitar warmth. Another mic can be placed back 5 feet or more in the studio for natural ambience, if desired. Here are my favorite mics, going up the price scale: Shure SM57, Audix OM3, Sennheiser E906 or 421, or a *large-diaphragm* studio condenser.

Though I prefer to mike, electric guitar can also be run directly to the mixer when using a guitar preamp, pedal, or multi-effect "pod" designed for this purpose. The problem is that optimal tone can often depend on the sound being processed and punched through a classic guitar amp and 12-inch speakers, particularly when it comes to distortion. Experiment. Direct or otherwise, you may find the unique sound that makes for an international star . . . or draws complaints from the neighbors.

Bass Guitar

I almost always favor running electric bass direct. There are rarely unforgiving effects to deal with, and you get accurate and isolated pickup of the instrument. Once in a great while in the studio, there comes along a bass rig that sounds so fantastic that it would be a sin not to let the rest of the world share in the experience. In those cases, I would most likely use my Audix D4 kick drum mic, the unique Tascam PE250 I've had for years (a secret tool in some studios), or a large-diaphragm condenser, and record it along with the direct track for added flexibility. If it's a good bass, this should be one of the easier instruments to capture well.

Drums

Drums are the toughest single undertaking for most engineers and require the most resources. And because drums collectively cover the broadest frequency range of any instrument, they share a place with vocals as one of the most crucial parts of your mix, studio or live. I suggest a minimum of six mics and a compatible mixer with at least three bands of ***EQ***, two sweepable, on each channel. (If you're already intimidated, it may be time to run out and buy an electronic drum set. You won't be the first, and I actually like some of the upscale electronic drums in smaller rooms where acoustic drum levels can be overwhelming.) If it's a less demanding application or you're a jazz purist, you're off the hook. Set up a stereo pair of good condensers over or just in front of the set and you'll get that natural sound. You can add an optional mic on the kick drum to individually control and accentuate it.

Individual drums require close miking to isolate them from each other and give more control of the mix. When the desired tone can't be achieved with the proper mic, placement, or drum tuning, it can be assisted by the mixer EQ. I'll offer some notes based on my drum miking experience and EQ techniques, which are discussed further in Chapter 5 if you get confused. After becoming more familiar with EQ itself, you may then wish to refer back to these notes. Or you may regard them as useless suggestions for what you're attempting to achieve. Your choice.

Many engineers use **_noise gates_** on mics to isolate drums, and sometimes they may be necessary. I prefer not to use them for several reasons. Most isolation problems can be controlled by mic choice, placement, and EQ. Also, some bleed through other mics can give the drums more of a live sound when balanced effectively. So don't feel it necessary to stock up on noise gates or activate all the internal ones in a digital mixer. Keep your focus first on good mics and their location.

In live sound, clear drum shields help significantly in reducing drum levels in the house and give the sound engineer more control over the drum mix. Use shields that are 5 feet high and, if there are hard walls behind the drums, provide acoustical wall treatment, curtains, or free-standing, sound-absorbing baffles behind the drums to cut down on reflections.

Kick Drum

The kick drum requires a specialized mic like an Audix D6 or AKG D112 to handle the excessive air pressure and low frequencies. Though you can certainly mike a drum head without a hole, it is usually best with the mic inside the shell and aimed toward the beater for a good, high-frequency attack. (Low-end without high-end punch is just a dull, chest-pumping thud—but then, some people like that.) If you need a bit more low-end punch, you can place the head of the mic just inside the hole to capture the air pressure at its exit point.

Some potential problem areas: excessive bass below 60Hz, muddiness in the 100–300Hz range, and/or a need for more attack around 2–4kHz. (I never mike the kick pedal side due to potential pedal noise and less isolation from snare and floor tom.)

Snare

Any of the mics listed for electric guitar (except the large studio condenser) and any drum-specific models are appropriate for snare. I avoid condensers because I think they make the snare sound too "brittle." A miking problem here might be bleed from the hi-hat, especially if the drummer likes to bang it partially open all the time or is crazy enough to use Rude cymbals. I minimize such bleed by pointing the mic away from the hat just over the edge of the snare under the first tom, and using a hypercardioid mic if necessary.

Placing the head of the mic near the edge allows better pickup of the shell and snares underneath. Placing it over the snare head will often result in more of a dull pop, which may force you to boost high end and increase hat bleed. Problems may be a dull or hollow bump in the 300–600Hz range or a need for a little more high end from 2–4kHz. In the studio, you could mike the bottom head as well to control snare balance if you feel it is really necessary.

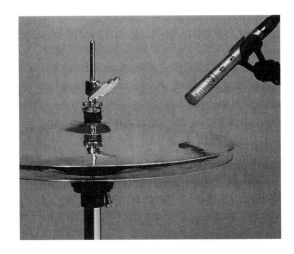

Hi-hat

Mike the hi-hat with a good condenser like Shure's SM81, a mini like their SM98, or an Audix M1255B pointing straight down a few inches above the outside edge opposite the drummer. Pointing it toward the drummer's side will pick up too much stick clicking. Isolation is generally not a problem, but I prefer to roll out all frequencies below 800Hz to eliminate the other drums and isolate the hat, and boost above 10kHz a touch if I need a sweeter high end.

Toms

Mike just over the outside edge, pointing across the head, with the same type of mic used for the snare. You may need to roll out some dullness in the 200–400Hz range or add a touch of 3–4kHz. If you have to pick up two toms with one mic, pick the smallest toms and use a cardioid mic with good low end. For a fatter sound on floor tom, I'll often use a kick drum mic to accentuate those lower frequencies.

If you use appropriate mini-condensers for rack toms, you can adjust their proximity (set them a little higher) to also pick up and balance adjacent cymbals, since condensers are less directional and reproduce better high end. You also have some additional balance control with their channel EQ by adjusting 4kHz and up for cymbals, and 500Hz on down for the toms. This can work well when you are short of mics or channels, and stereo panning for the toms also pans the cymbals accordingly.

Overheads

Use a good condenser in the middle of the set about a foot above the highest cymbal. If two mics are available, use a stereo pair angled out toward opposite groups of cymbals. I roll out everything below 200Hz to keep the low end tight on the drums. Frequencies up to 500Hz may also be cut to maximize cymbal pickup and minimize ambient pickup of the overall set. In smaller live venues, you can often eliminate overheads since the cymbals will carry and may get picked up by vocal mics anyway (absent a drum shield, of course).

If you use electronic drums, I recommend splitting off at least kick, snare, hi-hat, and the rest of the set through four different outputs on the sound module so the house engineer has independent control of these crucial elements, like with an acoustic set. I can handle the "rest of the set" through one channel since high and low EQ can control some balance between cymbals and toms that may be a little off in the drum module itself. Many electronic sets have this output capability, and I would make it a priority in a purchase.

Percussion

Use the same overhead-style miking for separate percussion setups. Dynamic mics will do fine for stronger instruments like congas, bongos, and cowbells. Live setups can also be picked up with a good lapel mic, wired or wireless, on the percussionist himself, providing a mic that moves with him to the various instruments. From the chest location, point the lapel element downward toward the instruments instead of upward, especially if it's a unidirectional mic.

Acoustic Piano

This is a large instrument, so trust your ears and listen around the instrument soundboard for the sweet spots. A safe and accurate bet in solo grand piano recording is a stereo pair of condenser mics placed 3–5 feet away with the piano lid fully open. Of course, with the distance, room acoustics are going to be a more significant aspect of the sound, which can be good or bad depending on the room. If you don't have access to a good room or you simply need more isolation, you can mike inside about a foot high over each side of the soundboard for even pickup. If the mics are too low, the strings closest to the elements will peak on

you. If you desire a brighter sound with more attack, move mics closer to the hammers. (For isolation in a group performance, position loud instruments like drums and brass farther away from the piano.)

In live sound and especially with loud bands, I've found a reasonably balanced sound and good isolation from a single unidirectional condenser if the grand is a 7–9-footer. With the lid at the lowest open position, place the mic on a boom over the strings about halfway in from either side. Experiment a little with placement directly over internal bracing in that area since it acts as a slight dividing line between different ranges of strings. The mic should be as close to the lid as possible without touching, parallel to the soundboard, and pointing toward the back end with the rear of the mic near the hammers. This works because the mic is directed to the back to maximize bass and warmth, while the normally peaky mids and highs are off axis (to the side) and rejected for a smoothing and balancing effect. It's not as effective with a smaller grand, which may lack enough warmth and bass to balance with the high strings. Some EQ may still be necessary to compensate for low-mid resonance off the soundboard and lid. This is usually cut a bit somewhere between 250Hz and 400Hz.

Though standmount condensers are always best, a flat condenser *boundary* mic like the Audio-Technica U851R attached to the piano lid will work okay, and placing it well may even allow you to close the lid completely and still get a pretty balanced sound. There are also high-end kits available for piano, like the DPA 4099P, Earthworks' PianoMic System, and Audix SCX25A with optimized mic pairs and accessories—they run $1,000 to $3,000, but they are a good investment if the grand piano ends up being a significant part of your efforts.

With spinets and uprights, I've never gotten an acceptable sound miking from the top (though you might want to try it), and miking from the front often picks up too much pedal noise. So I find it more effective to mike from the rear. Usually the second opening in the frame from the bass side gives me a decent sound with a single mic pointing right into the rear soundboard. For stereo, just find a good spot toward the other end. Frankly, most of these pianos sound pretty unimpressive, so I'd opt for a good electronic keyboard if a grand isn't available.

Orchestra

To capture that natural quality I keep referring to, orchestral or band instruments should be miked from at least 1 foot away, and ensembles or sections at least 3 feet away. The distance also minimizes the "edginess" of strings and the mechanical noises of some instruments. In performances, isolation doesn't take priority over proper mic placement, and some ambience or bleed can actually add dimension. The greater concern is to keep louder instruments, such as percussion and brass, away from the softer and lesser-projecting instruments, like piano and strings.

In recording, you could just stereo mike the room to capture a performance as the audience hears it and eliminate mixing altogether. But close miking allows for subtle and individual control of sections where needed and as a producer may prefer. For live solo instruments in bands or ensembles, there are also a number of small, clip-on mic designs, both wired and wireless.

Strings

Like acoustic guitar, other stringed instruments are also relatively low level and require the most consideration in pickup and isolation, so always use a good condenser. For a single violin, viola, cello, or string bass, point the mic toward the bridge and *f*-hole area. For ensembles, center the mic over the group and angle it slightly away from louder instrument sections if necessary. Treat harp like an acoustic guitar and mike from the side and slightly above the soundboard where it sounds balanced.

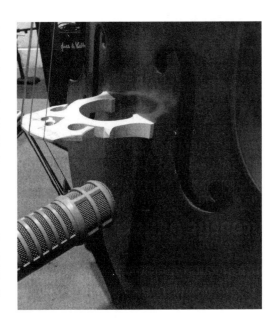

Woodwinds

For isolating one or two instruments, you can mike near the end or bell. With ensembles, center in front of the group at an appropriate distance to pick them all up. Flutes, oboes, and bassoons should be miked from above. Good dynamic mics will do okay for small groups of two or three.

Brass

Dynamics will often suffice here, but a condenser will cover a larger section. Since horns are more directional, be sure to get enough distance on sections for a good blend of the whole group. French horn can be miked from above and behind. (So why do they stick their fist in the bell? I think they're stashing something in there.)

Orchestral Percussion

Due to the extreme frequency ranges involved—from timpani to bells and cymbals, always use condensers. I can usually cover the whole section with one or two mics at a slight distance, so I tend to concentrate placement on making sure I get a full sound on timpani; the high-end stuff usually cuts through.

Vocals

Most of the microphones made are designed with vocals in mind, so there's no shortage of choices here, including hands-free headmic models. (We'll cover the various versions and differences in Chapter 3, "Unplugged.") There is often little need to worry about mic placement since the performer is going to eat

the mic anyway. Just hook them up, spread on some barbecue sauce, and set 'em loose. The rest, God willing, will be done at the mixer. On the other hand, if someone is holding the mic at waist level or waving it around in hand gestures as they speak (yes, I have had people do that), you will have to teach them some mic technique.

In the studio, you'll have more immediate control of mic technique. Definitely use a good condenser and try to keep the performer at least 3 inches away by using a nylon pop screen set in front of the mic to maintain distance and minimize breath pops. If the mic has a low roll-off switch, use it to further reduce low-end muddiness or pops.

Harmony

There are two ways to mike harmony parts. One, as you have probably already figured out, is to mike each singer, giving you the most isolation and total control of the mix. In multitrack recording, these can be recorded simultaneously or overdubbed one voice at a time to allow singers to concentrate on their individual parts. Another acceptable way is to use one cardioid mic for multiple singers (maximum three per mic). In live situations with a good vocal ensemble, this will allow them to control most of their blend naturally, so they can't blame you for the balance.

In the studio, I often prefer a stereo pair setup for ensembles because it gives me the natural dimensional imaging of everybody being in a unique position in that stereo field due to placement and room ambience—something you can't simulate with effects. I can wrap up to 10 singers in a semicircle around the two mics. The biggest problem is when singers just aren't proficient enough to perform their parts well together. Then it's back to one track at a time.

Choir

This is more of a problem due to the sheer number of people and their distance from the mics. Always use unidirectional condensers. With the availability of more economical miniature hanging or standmount choir mics, it isn't essential to buy the more expensive studio condensers for live use, which sometimes can be a disadvantage because their sensitive pickups are more prone to feedback and extraneous noises.

I space out one mic for every four or five people across, two or three rows deep. (More rows may require additional rear mics, or just stick all the bad singers in the back and don't worry about it.) Assuming you're about 6 feet tall, stand on the first row and stretch your arm up in front of you at a 45° angle. Place the mic head just beyond your fingertips and pointing at the back rows. This method gets the mic closer to the overall source, picks up the back rows on axis, and slightly rejects the closer front row which would otherwise tend to be louder.

For more forgiving sound situations, such as recording or when you're not competing with orchestra or band levels, you may be able to cut the number of mics in half or use a stereo pair, and place them at a greater distance to capture the overall natural balance. Miking options can include gooseneck podium mics on stands (which use the same elements as the miniature hanging mics) and the Audix MicroBoom series, which offers an excellent mic integrated onto a thin boom with internal cabling. For picking up smaller ensembles upstage or on front steps, good wireless handhelds on stands can be used to avoid a tripping hazard from cables along the floor.

If you're having trouble getting choir over full band and/or orchestra, try wireless handhelds or "invisible" mini-headworn mics on eight to ten primary singers. Be careful to blend their sound so they don't stand out as soloists. (Of course, you can always raise level for a solo.) Omnidirectional headworns are a plus here because they will pick up a little from adjacent singers for a more natural blend.

Remember, miking choir is about density of sound. If people are spread out too wide, it will be harder to pick them up. So for 30 people, it is better to have three rows of 10 instead of two rows of 15 to focus more sound into the mics. Like photography, focusing equals clarity.

Podium

Condensers come in several designs for this purpose, including goosenecks from 12 to 18 inches long and hemispherical boundary mics. One quick note: most of these small condensers are not designed with close pickup in mind and can be overloaded by powerful voices within 6 inches. Unless you prefer the sound quality of a heavy metal band through a Radio Shack PA and the wind noise of a category 3 hurricane (even with a windscreen on it), consider substituting a quality handheld in situations where pastors or others tend to eat the podium mic.

I spent a lot of time on mic choice and use because that's where it all starts. If you screw up here, you'll never fully recover later on. Mic technique is a commonsense art and will make everything else easier if done right.

A final point would be to use mics like a light. Do you need a floodlight to cover a wide area? Do you need a narrower spot beam to project a little farther into the darkness? Where would you point it to best illuminate everything evenly? Mic pickup works the same in reverse: *omnidirectional* = lightbulb, *cardioid* = floodlight, *hypercardioid* = medium spot, *supercardioid* = narrow spot. See the light?

Unplugged

THE WONDERFUL WORLD OF WIRELESS

Hop on down to the local music store, pick out an economical wireless mic, hook it up to your sound system, and let the fun begin! Unfortunately, as with many technological tools, it's not always that easy. Nobody promised audio geeks a rose garden, but my initial experiences even fell short of compost!

My introduction to wireless systems was back in the '80s, when we were subjected to primitive, low-cost VHF, which, at that time, performed horribly. I naturally assumed that poor quality, annoying noises, signals dropping out, and frequent breakdowns were unavoidable aspects of wireless, and I lost faith until some good wireless (VHF and UHF) showed up in the $1,500 range. Finally we were getting decent performance, though such cost was still prohibitive for many who needed these convenient tools—especially churches and community theatres that required multiple systems. The good news is that better UHF is now the standard, and prices for dependable wireless systems have come down while quality has consistently improved.

Nonetheless, unexpected problems arose as I combined multiple units, used them in different environments, and integrated them into various systems. So began my quest for solutions based on research, trial and error, and numerous soul-stirring revelations—usually preceded by incredible stupidity. This chapter is a byproduct intended to help you get more out of wireless microphones and bring you up to date on some features, price ranges, and potential problems to avoid or overcome.

Maybe it's just me, but I trust the top wired microphone manufacturers to produce the best wireless. I believe they give more attention to details that maintain the sonic integrity of their mics. In fact, it is not just the mic element that affects the sound, but the mic casing as well. The original manufacturer is more likely to assure their wireless casing is designed accordingly. AKG, Audio-Technica, Audix, Beyer, Sennheiser, and Shure top the list, and all of these companies have done a good job of improving features and performance over the years. Here's some things I look for (or hope for) in a wireless system:

1. Though the standard receiver chassis need not come rackmount, all should be rackmountable with rack accessories included. Rackmounting reduces abuse and possible damage to units and their connections and offers security and convenient transport for multiple systems. The receivers should also be designed with a flat top for easy and stable vertical stacking when not rackmounted. A metal chassis is preferred over plastic.

2. Receiver output should be line level for better signal-to-noise ratio, especially when patched through longer lines or snakes. Mic-level outputs are simply not necessary with the input flexibility of current

mixers, and a simple variable-level control on the output can accommodate lower gain inputs. There should be both 1/4-inch phone and balanced XLR connections and a related ground lift switch to eliminate *ground loop* hums.

3. Though most of the mic companies listed above offer optional power distribution units for multiple systems, a lot of the economical receivers still use AC adapters ("wall warts") for their power to save on cost. If you have to have them, they should utilize a slim design that will work in standard power strips without blocking other outlets so you can easily power more systems without the extra expense of distribution. (Aviom's PS-120 is just such a design used for their multichannel in-ear devices.)

4. Lapel mics (and other applications that necessitate a cable) possess the greatest failure potential due to cable stress at the belt-pack connection. Manufacturers should use a right angle plug instead of straight to eliminate the sharp "U-turn" of the dangling cable. An option for straight plugs is a connection on the underside of the beltpack instead of the top so the cable can hang straight. Thankfully, many transmitter packs have a metal belt clip that can be flipped upside down so the connection *can* be on the bottom. Look for this feature. (This may orient switches and indicators on the bottom too, but that's no big deal.) And wouldn't it be lovely if all the wireless manufacturers adopted a standard mic connector for compatibility and interchangeability with all packs? Hint, hint . . .

STRESS→

5. Transmitters should be easy to switch on, and there should be continuous "active" indication as opposed to the instantaneous LED blink of some systems. Even better is the battery meter now provided in many transmitter LCD displays that is also duplicated on the receiver so the soundman can keep an eye on battery levels. All transmitters should have silent on/off, not the annoying "thump" still evident on some units, and many now have an on/off locking feature. This is useful for avoiding accidental shutoff in theatrical productions when some performers want to toy with the switches.

A WIRELESS OVERVIEW

Take a microphone and hook it up to its own miniature radio station, and you have a wireless mic system. This is composed of a battery-operated transmitter, which the mic is connected to, and a receiver that receives the transmitted signal and passes it on to the mixer inputs. Just as radio stations must transmit on different frequency channels, you need a different channel for each wireless mic system to operate multiples simultaneously.

All wireless mics can emit some "spurious" **RF** (radio frequencies) that may interfere with each other. These are much weaker than their transmitting frequencies and usually don't cause a problem when transmitters are at normal working distances from the receivers. But you may notice interference and/or signal indication on more than one receiver when a lone transmitter is switched on within a few feet of them. A little distance, say 10 feet or more, and the problem should go away since those spurious signals are too weak to carry far. Simply speaking, the more systems you run, the more the air can get cluttered with these frequencies and receivers can get confused as to who their partner is. (Sounds like Hollywood, doesn't it?)

Earlier **VHF**, or **V**ery **H**igh **F**requency, wireless systems used the 169MHz to 216MHz frequency range. Manufacturers generally offered about 15 to 20 VHF channels, but it was important to avoid TV and FM radio channels in the local area that could interfere. VHF is rarely used today due to the tighter reception and affordability of UHF but can still work well if you have a good one lying around. I have a couple I've held onto for small gigs, one for a headworn mic and another for an acoustic guitar so I don't have to lug my rack of UHF around. I also don't have to worry about it competing with nearby UHF.

UHF, or **U**ltra **H**igh **F**requency, systems currently run from around 500MHz through 600MHz and 900MHz to 2.4GHz.

(Note: The 700MHz range has been banned from wireless use by the FCC. Though more bands may face restrictions, the ranges above should be relatively safe for a while.)

UHF offers much tighter reception, allowing many more systems to be used, and with fewer interference problems. In fact, Broadway shows may use 32 or more! (The battery budget alone must rival what the government pays for a hammer.) Most UHF mics also provide user-switchable tuning, so you can change to another frequency if a problem arises with one. Good UHF systems are now equal to the cost of former VHF, starting at around $300. I'll warn you that I have never gotten decent performance from any wireless system costing less than $300 new, including from major name brands.

The farther away the transmitters and receivers are from each other, the weaker the signal gets. Problems arise from sheer distance or when original and reflected signals arrive at an antenna simultaneously, canceling each other out and resulting in noise or loss of audio. Where earlier **non-diversity** (single-antenna) VHF suffered from this the most, current UHF wireless mics employ **diversity** (dual-antenna) circuits that improve reception by detecting when an antenna starts to lose signal and switching to the other antenna circuit without any conspicuous break in the audio.

Some receivers have a **squelch** (or **mute**) control that can be adjusted to block weaker frequencies (and related noise) that try to butt in when signal is lost or the transmitter is cut off. I find that squelch is usually adjusted properly at the factory, so I don't recommend messing with it unless you are a pro. (I'll discuss other ways to address interference problems in the Troubleshooting section of this chapter.)

Other typical receiver features include meters for **RF** signal strength and **Audio** for levels and peaks, plus an output level control. Both transmitters and receivers have frequency selection (typically anywhere from 10 to over 1,000 frequencies), and the nice LCD displays on many systems today provide a lot of extra features, including a battery strength meter, auto-search for clear frequency settings, and convenient naming of each system.

If a system doesn't have a naming feature, I often tune available frequencies displayed so the last whole number "labels" the unit, such as 561.0MHz, 562.0MHz, and 563.0MHz for wireless 1, 2, and 3. It's just an easy way to keep track of them if the consecutive frequencies don't suffer any interference issues.

Wireless **lapels** are "tie clip" style mics used primarily for speaking and theatre, though they can also be effective for some creative miking, including acoustic guitar and percussion (which I talked about in the last chapter).

Lapel systems use a battery-operated belt pack for the electronics and transmitter. Mics are available in omnidirectional and unidirectional models. Most people think that, as with handheld mics, a unidirectional pattern is best for lapels because it is less prone to *feedback*. However, due to the typical chest placement of lapel mics, there ends up being little difference in the feedback potential between omni and uni patterns, but considerable difference in the way they perform.

Since unidirectionals are designed to reject distant and off-axis pickup to reduce feedback and background sounds, lapel placement ends up rejecting the voice as well necessitating increased gain to restore vocal level. As a result, feedback potential is increased, especially in the higher frequencies, and the gain at the mic element itself can be up to three times louder than an omni in the same position. This makes the unidirectional much more subject to noises such as breath or wind, rubbing of clothing, or microphonic noise from the cable itself. (If you ever hear a pastor's broadcast with a lot of extraneous breath or clothing noise, you know the soundman made the mistake of using a unidirectional lapel.) A final problem with these mics at the chest location is their greater tendency to lose voice level when the user turns his head, another shortcoming of rejection. The solution: *use an omnidirectional.* You will get better gain, a fuller sound, and a more consistent level.

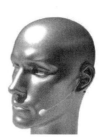

Wireless **handhelds** have self-contained transmitters in their handles, and **headmics** use a belt pack module like lapel systems. As with handhelds, headmics used for singing and louder music levels will be unidirectional and mounted next to or in front of the mouth, but mic placement is crucial since slight changes in position can alter the sound significantly. They also require substantial windscreens to avoid breath pops. For pastors, public speaking, and theatre, this makes them much more conspicuous and bulky than the omnidirectional "near invisible" mini-headmics, which now offer alternate choices in both single and dual earloop styles.

It has always made more sense for a head-mounted speaking mic to be omnidirectional, like a lapel. There is little need for isolation from loud music, an omni element can be much smaller since it requires no unidirectional vents, and it suffers no proximity effect. It can be positioned at the side of the face (away from the mouth), so it requires no bulky windscreen to avoid breath pop, and unlike lapel mics, it follows the head movement while sitting much closer to the mouth.

Just to clarify some jargon, **single earloop** models hang over one ear, and **dual earloop** models hang over both ears with a band around the back of the head. The latter are more stable and secure for animated movement. (Of course, you can tape down single-ear models with a little clear surgical tape when needed to keep them from shifting.) Popular mini-headmics are made by Audio-Technica, Countryman, DPA, and Sennheiser, to name a few. I've also used a decent and cheaper model from Airwave called the Slimline. Most headmics can be ordered in different colors and with a variety of connector plugs for compatibility with any of the major-brand wireless belt packs.

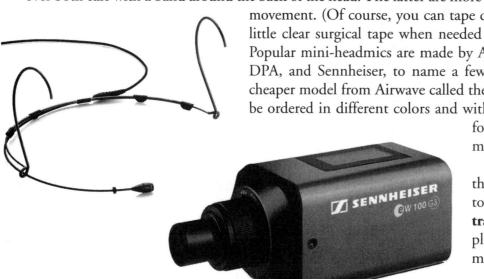

Lectrosonics and Azden were the first wireless manufacturers to offer a small **plug-on transmitter** module that would plug into the base of any normal mic and turn it into a wireless.

Now several companies offer these plug-ons for their systems, including Shure and Sennheiser models (also with phantom power). These even provide enough input gain adjustment to handle line-level signals, so you can also use them for wireless transmission of other XLR feeds, such as a portable mixer to an amp rack or broadcast booth.

Now think about the possibilities. I once used a plug-on transmitter in a church on a miniature podium condenser mic for cable-free operation of a pulpit in the middle of an open floor. (The module has to provide phantom power, or you'll need a battery-operated podium mic.) I also used a plug-on to successfully transmit a feed from a sanctuary mixer to a sound system in a separate social hall building for remote listening, but I custom-wired the module's battery contacts to an appropriate AC adapter to eliminate the need for changing batteries. Yes, new wireless innovations challenge us to be innovative, but I sometimes go a little wild!

TROUBLESHOOTING

Reception

The first concern with wireless setup is making sure you get strong and consistent reception of the mics. Older single-antenna (nondiversity) VHF systems were only dependable indoors within a 50-foot range between transmitter and receiver, while dual-antenna (diversity) systems typically allow a 75- to 100-foot range—in spite of the fact that some specs tell you they're good for 200 feet to a quarter of a mile. Of course, this is under perfect conditions: outdoors at the Bonneville Salt Flats on a clear day with no sunspot activity. Any concerts there recently?

I prefer to set up receivers at my mixer location so I can know when the transmitters are active and see the RF strength, but there have been some situations where I placed receivers near the stage and ran their signals through an audio snake due to problems with space limitations, distance, or potential interference from digital audio or multimedia equipment at the mix position. (More about that later.) The main concern here was having the extra lines from the stage and making sure they were **balanced** connections, either available as XLR outputs on the receiver or by using a **direct box**.

Always place receivers for maximum reasonable elevation. Balcony locations, usually in churches or theaters, obviously offer the best elevation and unobstructed line of sight to transmitters. Set one antenna vertical and a second angled, or experiment with antenna angles if you have a minor dropout problem. Also, with some belt-pack transmitters, the mic cable doubles as an antenna, so make sure it is relatively straight and not bundled or coiled up while in use. I'll run you through a series of reception checks in the next section.

Interference

This stuff can be mysterious. Sometimes interference sounds like erratic distortion, noise, or static. Sometimes it sounds like mic feedback, though it's distinguished by multiple tones that fade in and out and are not constant like feedback. It can also result in a pop or momentary static when the transmitter is cut off, the effect of instantaneous interference before the receiver has a chance to auto-mute after losing its primary signal.

In any case, interference happens when the receiver is trying to receive another renegade signal from somewhere else, either when the transmitter's signal is lost or weak or when the stray signal is just too strong on that particular frequency. Though it can be caused by other wireless mics, offenders also include radio and TV broadcast frequencies, power transformers, digital equipment such as CD players/recorders, digital mixers and lighting boards, computers, video gear, keyboards, and effects units. I've also had situations where wireless systems of mixed brands and frequency settings interfered with each other, and a system in a church at the other end of the block was being picked up 500 feet away! (If this occurs, it would be helpful for both of you to meet and coordinate on some frequency settings prior to implementing combat radio-jamming strategies.) For all these problems, here are a few preventives or quick fixes to consider:

TV CHANNEL	21	22	23	24	25	26	27	28	29	30
Frequency Range	470-478MHz	478-486MHz	486-494MHz	494-502MHz	502-510MHz	510-518MHz	518-526MHz	526-534MHz	534-542MHz	542-550MHz
TV CHANNEL	31	32	33	34	35	36	37	38	39	40
Frequency Range	550-558MHz	558-566MHz	566-574MHz	574-582MHz	582-590MHz	590-598MHz	598-606MHz	606-614MHz	614-622MHz	622-630MHz
TV CHANNEL	41	42	43	44	45	46	47	48	49	50
Frequency Range	630-638MHz	638-646MHz	646-654MHz	654-662MHz	662-670MHz	670-678MHz	678-686MHz	686-694MHz	694-702MHz	702-710MHz
TV CHANNEL	51	52	53	54	55	56	57	58	59	60
Frequency Range	710-718MHz	718-726MHz	726-734MHz	734-742MHz	742-750MHz	750-758MHz	758-766MHz	766-774MHz	774-782MHz	782-790MHz
TV CHANNEL	61	62	63	64	65	66	67	68	69	70
Frequency Range	790-798MHz	798-806MHz	806-814MHz	814-822MHz	822-830MHz	830-838MHz	838-846MHz	846-854MHz	854-862MHz	863-865MHz

Interleaved Spectrum available for wireless microphones and IEM's now and post DSO 2012.

Channels 38-40 available for wireless microphones and IEM's on a shared licence basis after January 4th, 2010.
Channel 38 is available nationwide (expected 21.09.2011, channels 39-40 will be part of interleaved spectrum.

First, avoid wireless systems that transmit on local DTV broadcast frequencies. You should be able to get listings or info in the owner's manual, on the manufacturer's website, or by calling or emailing the manufacturer. It is really a responsibility of the wireless dealers to collaborate with manufacturers on providing systems appropriate to your area, and to make sure any multiple systems you might be adding onto are compatible. But you can avoid problems by raising the issue to ensure that dealers don't sell you problem frequencies, and that they will swap a system if you have problems. User-switchable channels are clearly an advantage whether used locally or on the road.

The first step in determining interference problems is to power up systems without transmitters on and see if any of their RF meters indicate reception. If so, begin cutting off nearby equipment one at a time, especially digital equipment, to see if the RF indicator goes out or at least drops to only one bar, which is usually insignificant. You may find that your CD player or digital mixer is causing the problem. Once the culprit is found, you can move them farther apart, switch frequency, or, if the receiver has adjustable-length antennae, drop  them down one or two sections from the top. (This can act like a squelch by weakening signal reception and, unlike squelch, continues to avoid the offender even when the transmitter is on.) You just want to make sure the antenna adjustment doesn't lose your mic transmitter once it is at normal working distance.

Once outside problems are eliminated, it's time to check transmitters one at a time. As each one is cut on, take note if its signal is picked up on more than its own receiver (the RF indicator again). This can be caused when transmitters are close to all the receivers and will typically disappear when the transmitters are farther away during normal use. If the problem doesn't go away, you will need to switch frequencies.

If incompatibilities remain, you may need to replace that system. This is more common with older systems or mismatched brands. As a result, it is often better to stick with one manufacturer when combining multiple systems unless the brands are purchased in totally different frequency ranges.

Once the transmitters are being properly received, check reception at your maximum working distance from the receivers. If you start getting dropouts, try eliminating them by

checking batteries, adjusting antenna extension and angles, or elevating the receivers. If this doesn't work, you may need to purchase an antenna distribution unit with directional paddles for better reception, or simply move the receivers closer to the transmitters. Be mindful of the possibility for interference from nearby wireless if you are in a convention hall or meeting facility, near another church, etc. The unlikelihood of identical frequencies and the sheer distance alone are usually sufficient insurance, but it is always wise to be ready for potential problems.

Gain Settings

Setting proper levels on gain and volume controls allows you to get a good, clear signal without distortion. *Gain*, or **sensitivity**, normally implies level *into* a device, where volume or level is output *from* a device.

Transmitters have a gain control within an LCD display menu or somewhere on the casing or in the battery compartment as a recessed screw-type adjustment. But don't fret about having to make immediate adjustments because, most of the time, gain is set pretty well from the factory.

Receivers have an audio level control for their outputs, and I normally set this all the way up for the strongest signal and lowest noise to my mixer and so they can't be accidentally cranked up and cause feedback or overload my mixer settings. Mixers have input gain control and usually peak level indication on each channel to let you know if a receiver output is too strong. You'll need to adjust the mixer's channel gain to the point where the peak indicator does not flash during the loudest signals from the wireless. If your mixer does not have sufficient gain control and/or a **pad** button on the channel, you will need to back off on the receiver level if you notice distortion or a mixer channel going into the red. (More on this later in Chapter 6.)

The sensitivity setting on the transmitter serves the same purpose. If level is too strong from a powerful voice or instrument, the signal can distort. Unlike mixer settings, you can't make a quick transmitter adjustment once things get going, so you'll want to make sure this is properly set ahead of time for the strongest possible vocalist or designated instrument. All you need to do is have the user speak, sing, or play at their loudest level and see if you notice any distortion in the sound or peak indication on the transmitter or receiver. If not, leave the sensitivity at the factory setting. If you do notice distortion or peak indication, simply lower the transmitter sensitivity slightly

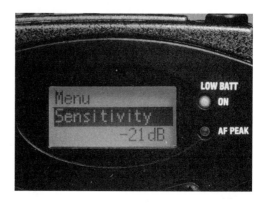

until distortion ceases or peak indication doesn't light. For those receivers with an actual audio meter, adjust the transmitter sensitivity so that the loudest signals just barely reach peak level. This will assure low-noise operation since some receivers exhibit inherent noise if the mixer channel is cranked up to compensate for a low transmitter signal. Check your owner's manual for specific adjustment details.

Equalization

Recommending *EQ* (or tone) settings for your wireless is a little touchy because it depends on the mic you're using, the sound quality of your speakers, and proper equalization of the sound system itself. I can offer some appropriate suggestions for certain mics based on an accurate system, which should at least get you headed in the right direction. In regard to the following notes, I refer you again to Chapter 6 ("Virtual Plumbing 201") for an in-depth discussion on EQ adjustments, including **sweep EQ,** which can be essential here.

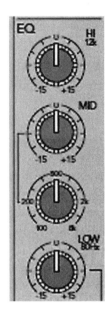

Handhelds are not much of a problem through a properly tuned system. The prime concern is the proximity effect of unidirectionals. When the performer is speaking or singing from more than 6 inches away from the mic, you can leave the low-end EQ level at the 11:00 to 12:00 position. *Do not boost low end for vocals because it can make the sound muddy or boomy.* As people get closer to the mic, you'll need to decrease the low end a notch or two more. The same applies for **unidirectional headmics**, along with controlling some potential high-end "edge" from their smaller condenser elements. If this is too pronounced, you'll need to set the mid-sweep frequency knob somewhere between 3kHz and 6.3kHz and back off the associated mid-gain control to the 11:00 or 10:00 position, depending on how harsh the "edge" is.

Lapel mics have always been more of a problem then headmics due to their off-axis location, requiring more level and EQ adjustment to pick up the voice clearly without feedback. Unidirectional lapels tend to sound thinner due to loss of low end from distance (proximity effect in reverse), and will typically have more feedback problems in the high end from 2kHz to 8kHz. Unfortunately, EQ adjustments to take out this problem can also diminish vocal clarity in the same high-end ranges. This clarity is one of the most important aspects of lapel performance because, in most rooms, the mic works in conjunction with the natural projection of ambient low and low-mid sound from the voice itself. Without this clarity, the voice sounds muddy from a distance, lacking the supplemental detail necessary for everyone to hear clearly. So with unidirectional lapels, you may get caught between feedback and maintaining vocal clarity.

Omnidirectional lapels don't suffer as much from gain loss or "reverse proximity effect." Their sonic surplus is in the lower frequencies, which can be accentuated by the mic picking up chest resonance. (Put your ear to someone's chest while they're speaking and you'll know what I mean. This is best not performed on strangers.) As a result, you need to decrease specific low and low-mid frequencies, which, fortunately, does not affect the clarity range. Depending on the user's vocal tone, I might start by backing off low EQ to the 10:00 or 9:00 position to reduce muddiness while taking care not to make the voice sound too thin.

The low-mid problem occurs at around 400Hz to 600Hz, causes a "hollow" muddiness, is most prone to feedback, and falls within a *resonance frequency* of most rooms. This resonance from sound bouncing off walls actually amplifies the problem and makes the sound even muddier and more reverberant. Reducing these frequencies not only clears up the sound but diminishes its bouncing around in the room. I would start at around 560Hz and reduce the associated mid-gain control to the 10:00 or even 9:00 position. You can then readjust the midsweep back and forth a little if needed, to the point at which you get the least low-mid feedback and the sound is clearest and most pleasing. Once these ranges are under control, you should have some room to bring up high end if needed. Some lapels may require a slight boost at around 2kHz to 2.5kHz, which can help increase level and clarity on a soft or muffled voice.

Obviously, controlling specific frequencies can be a problem if you don't have midsweep EQ. But if you have a 4-band *fixed* EQ, you can still use the sweep EQ recommendations because you will have a low-mid knob usually fixed somewhere in the 400–500Hz range to cut the same muddiness targeted with the sweep EQ.

Omnidirectional headmic adjustments are similar to a lapel, though you won't need the same degree of adjustment. Normally, you won't have to boost high end since the mic is closer to the voice, and the 400–600Hz gain will be cut less, if at all, to retain the warmth and fullness in the voice.

Batteries

I once asked a major theatrical engineer if she used rechargeables for her shows. She said, "You don't trust a $10,000,000 show to anything but a fresh alkaline." Though you probably are not in a multimillion-dollar production, this advice may be appropriate to the importance you place on your task. Still, people often ask about rechargeables, so here's my take on them.

Most wireless mics and packs have transitioned from 9V to AA alkalines, which you can find at specialty battery outlets online and even locally for less than 30 cents apiece. Where alkalines will give you 6–10 hours on most newer wireless systems, good rechargeables usually last only 2–4 hours, and they require following a regimen of battery recharging and rotation. If you do get rechargeables, nickel metal hydride (NiMH) are the only ones to use because they don't develop a "memory" if they're partially drained for a routine period and then recharged. Nickel cadmium batteries (NiCad) will quickly lose their maximum duration, dying at or before the end of even a short "memorized" routine period. Also, some brands don't actually reach full peak voltage with a recharge (maybe only 8V for a 9V battery), and I've seen some that drop in peak voltage with each recharge.

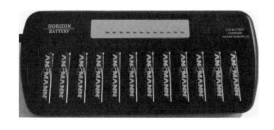

I've had good success with Ansmann AA and 9V rechargeable systems distributed by Horizon Battery, Full Compass, and BH Photo. The sophisticated multichargers drain, condition, and recharge their batteries for optimal life and performance. They even have pro rackmount chargers, but those are very expensive, unlike their consumer tabletop models. (The 12-bay pictured sells for $65.) I only use their longest-life batteries, the 2850mAh in AA and 300mAh in 9V (current as of this printing).

Another note: I now keep specific rechargeables mated with certain mic models. In my experience, once the batteries get used to the voltage drain of one type of mic, they may not last as long for others. For instance, the AAs may give me over 4 hours in one model of wireless handheld, but if I use them in another model, which should give me at least 3 hours, I may be lucky to get 1 hour out of those same batteries. Weird. (It seems even rechargeables can become prejudiced.)

I have enough rechargeables to run a full complement on stage for a normal Sunday service while another full set is recharging, but I always use alkalines for special events like concerts, conferences, and drama productions since those may run longer than expected. If you're worried about any of the above concerns or procedures, stick with alkalines.

It's a good idea to check all batteries with a voltage meter before you use them, since even new alkalines can be defective. Thankfully, many UHF systems now have battery meters in transmitter *and* receiver displays (I love that!) to check levels and keep track so you aren't tossing batteries that still have a decent

life. I've found that alkalines in some mic models that have dropped to a 2-hour meter indication will show good for 3 or more hours in another model. In other words, the meters are based on that particular mic's power consumption, so their battery meters are a more accurate gauge. I also like it when pastors power their wireless on and off as they need it. It saves on battery life but also allows his mic channel to be up and ready so a soundman doesn't miss cues and force the pastor to learn sign language.

Another potential problem can be battery contacts. Be aware that batteries can be slightly different in size, so stick to one brand as much as possible. Nine-volt Duracells, for instance, are shorter than many other brands. If you use a longer battery and then swap to a shorter one, the battery contacts may be pushed back a bit too far for good connection. Contacts can also become dirty or oxidized from humidity or perspiration, so clean them periodically with tuner cleaner or alcohol. Some manufacturers offer gold-plated contacts to reduce the oxidation problem.

This chapter has addressed most of the wireless considerations and problems I've come across, and, hopefully, there won't be too many more popping up. Obviously, attention to detail minimizes the problems, but I still hold to one thought: If you don't need to be unplugged, plug. Wireless systems are an unparalleled convenience when you need the freedom, but cabled mics present lower costs and fewer concerns. Choose wisely. You'll find more under **Church Sound** and **Theatrical Sound** in Chapter 12.

Down To The Wire

4

CABLES

Now we're concerned with sending our source signals somewhere, so let's briefly touch on the subject of cables and connectors. Always keep in mind that signals flow like water: in one direction. (And for you smart guys who bring up phantom power, I'll say it's like salmon swimming upstream.) We're dealing with two types of signal travel determined by the mic or line output and input connections of our equipment—**balanced** and **unbalanced**. Storytime!

Imagine Mr. Guy Wire walking to the library when he gets followed by a large, hissing, snorting bully. Once Mr. Wire reaches the serene environment of his destination, he has brought along an uncontrollable and noisy deterrent to bibliophilic harmony. (You can look that up, 'cause I did.) Now imagine another scenario in which Mr. Wire meets his younger brother Trip at the library, both having been followed by bullies with equal antagonism and territorial tendencies. At the door, neither goon is willing to give way to the other, and they commence in a spirited altercation, ultimately leaving the brothers and library patrons inside in perfect peace.

Now stick with me on this. The brothers are your source signals traveling down a cable, the bullies are noise following along, and the library is your signal destination. The first example is an unbalanced cable with noise picked up along its length and no way to keep it from "getting in the door." The second example substitutes a balanced cable with an added "neutral" signal. Once at the destination, the undesirable noise introduced to both lines is filtered or phase-reversed to cancel itself out while leaving our desired signals unaffected. This is called **common mode rejection**. This is also called a **stretched analogy**.

Unbalancing Act

Unbalanced cables have two conductors: a **hot** (+) wire and a **ground** (–) or "shield" wire. The cable shield is wrapped around the hot wire to keep noise out, but there's a limit to its effectiveness. Noise is at relatively low levels but gets stronger as it accumulates over a cable's length. **Signal-to-noise** will determine how much of a problem this will cause and what we can get away with. Remember when we talked about source levels and *gain*? A microphone has a low level of around –60dB. If noise accumulates to –60dB over 100 feet of cable, it will be as loud as the signal. As a result, unbalanced high-impedance mic or guitar signals can't be sent through long cables. But a +4dB line level from a synthesizer or instrument preamp through the same 100-foot cable would yield a 64dB signal-to-noise difference, which may be enough to effectively mask noise. Therefore, those unbalanced line signals could feasibly get away with longer runs (though maybe not 100 feet) except for one other possibility—*ground loops*.

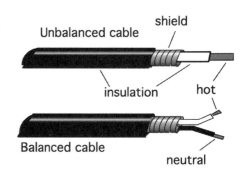

No, ground loops are not a new high-fiber cereal. They are hums caused by the signal cable ground of one AC-powered unit connected to another; more specifically, when they're plugged into different electrical wall circuits. So we would have to break the signal ground somehow to eliminate our final connection problem, and you can't do it with an unbalanced line because it will cut your audio. The good news is that balanced lines can help eliminate both noise and ground loops.

Balancing Act

Balanced cables have three conductors as illustrated: a **hot** (+), a **neutral** (−), and a **ground**. The hot and neutral both carry the signal circuit, so the ground can be cut at one end to eliminate a ground loop if one appears. The rule is to cut it at the input or receiving connector of a device. (You can also find in-line adapters that accomplish this *ground lift* for you.) Without even saying "abracadabra," all your noise problems will disappear and everyone will be in awe of your power. There have been occasions, though, when I was waiting for

the applause and suddenly realized that the noise was still there. This could indicate a problem with equipment or cables, incompatible chassis ground designs, or inherent noise in the source or electrical lines

(sometimes caused by lighting dimmers on the same circuit). Beginning at your sources, start cutting off or unplugging them one at a time, or possibly switching electrical outlets to determine or eliminate the problem. You may need to try a more sophisticated **hum eliminator** designed to tackle a range of annoying artifacts.

Another cute trick is eliminating a ground loop from an unbalanced output. As long as your destination is a *balanced* input, a cable can be made that connects the hot and ground of the unbalanced output cable to the hot and neutral of the destination input with the same results because the grounds of the two are not connected. More applause!

Direct Box

Unbalanced lines can be changed to balanced lines with a unit called a ***direct box***. This is a $10 balancing transformer that sells for $40 because musicians are suckers. It normally offers two 1/4-inch phone jacks and an XLR connector. Plug the instrument into one 1/4-inch jack and run a patch cable from the other to the instrument amp (if applicable) and a mic line from the XLR to the mixer. Most direct boxes also have a ground lift switch to break a ground loop. A direct box is especially necessary with low -level sources such as bass or guitar, but it should be used on any unbalanced sources having to traverse more than 30 feet of cable.

These connections are all used for mic and line sources and require shielded cables. You'll also find a great deal of these in a single, convenient, multi-cable package called a **snake** for running long distances. Speakers require larger-gauge cables with side-by-side wiring and some unique connectors. I'll elaborate on them later in the amplifier chapter.

CONNECTORS

There are only a few standard connectors used in audio, so I'll give a brief description of each and their wiring configurations:

1/4-inch phone plug

The most common, this is a two-conductor connector; tip = hot, sleeve = ground.

1/4-inch TRS phone plug

This is a three-conductor version with tip, ring, and sleeve connections; ring = neutral. (For balanced connections as well as stereo headphone plugs with Left, Right, and Ground connections. Another configuration for *inserts* will be discussed in the next chapter.)

RCA phono plug

This is a hi-fi-style, two-conductor connector; tip = hot, sleeve = ground. (Also used for coaxial digital audio connections.)

XLR male plug

The most popular three-conductor connector, the male version connects to inputs; three numbered pins are wired to an international standard: 1 = ground, 2 = hot, 3 = neutral.

XLR female plug

The female version commonly connects to outputs and has the same pin standard as the male. (Foreign manufacturers had previously designed equipment with XLRs wired pin 2 = neutral and pin 3 = hot. Check the manuals of older gear and consider having the equipment connector wiring corrected if it's not standard.)

I'd like to make note of unique solderless XLR plugs made by Alcatel, designated the AC3MI and AC3FI. Wiring supply companies like Horizon/Rapco have carried them and actually use dedicated machines that attach these plugs to cables, but I discovered that they are easily attached by hand. You need only strip 1 inch off the overall cable insulation (not the individual wires). The ground, hot, and neutral wires are then draped through slots numbered for them on the colored insert body, and the internal pin connector makes solid connection to each wire with stripping pins as the base is screwed on. They're easiest to use with 24-gauge mic cable but can work with 22-gauge too, and I've found them extremely reliable. If you do a lot of XLR in-line connectors, especially for multipair snake cables, try 'em. I can do 30 from scratch in less than half an hour and never heat up a soldering iron! Alcatel even got cute and made the internal body blue for XLR male and pink for XLR female. Kudos for more innovation.

One more thing—whenever I start having signal problems, static, a drop in levels, no audio, whatever, the first thing to check is connectors and cables. It can be as simple as dirty contacts or a broken wire at the stress point of the cable where it exits the connector. Nothing that a soldering iron or a little contact cleaner can't handle. Regular checks along with some routine unplugging and plugging to clean contacts won't hurt either. And it's a lot easier than fielding the complaints later.

Basic Plumbing 101

5

MIXERS

Now we get to the heart of the whole operation. The mixer will control almost everything from here on out and, consequently, is the most complex piece to use. All mixers have the same basic functions, but some have more features than others. The bigger the mixer, the more demanding its circuit design to keep accumulated electronic noise to a minimum, particularly with analog designs. A real cause for confusion with any mixer is the terminology. *Nobody* can seem to get together on what to call stuff! One man's gain is another man's trim, one lady's aux is another lady's send. I think this probably dates back to that Tower of Babel thing. Anyway, we'll cover the audio semantics along the way.

The next chapter, "Virtual Plumbing 201," will delve into the unique capabilities and operation of digital mixers. Right now I'm going to cover the basic features from an analog (nondigital) perspective. There are as many mixer designs as there are guitarists' egos, and I'm not inclined to elaborate

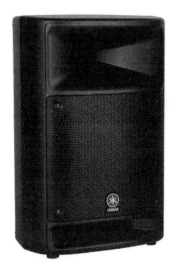

too heavily on either one. You will find the smaller units are usually box-style **powered mixers** with four to eight channels for under $1,000, or console-style with 8 to 16 channels under $2,000, all with the amplifier(s) built in. A few convenient package **portable systems,** like the Anchor Liberty, Fender Passport, and Yamaha Stagepas, are three- to six-channel all-in-one systems that include the speakers, too. **Unpowered mixers** with from 8 to 48 channels or more can run from less than $500 up into the stratosphere.

The first priority in choosing a mixer is how many sources you must accommodate. Always get at least a few extra channels for surprise needs. The next priority is how many aux sends you will need for stage monitoring, effects, recording, etc. I recommend at least four, though most larger mixers now come with 6 to 8 (for analog) and 8 to 16 (for digital). Any other considerations will usually be based on what you can afford and will determine how many bells and whistles you can reap in the process. Let's find out about some basic bells first.

EVERYTHING AND THE KITCHEN SINK

"Do you know what all those knobs do?" If I had a nickel for every time I was asked that question, I wouldn't be writing this book. Yes I do, and it's not that hard. Most of what you need to know is what one channel strip does. The rest just do the same thing for other sources. And each channel works just like your kitchen sink! Follow me on a pipe dream . . .

Gain: Check out the valve on one of your pipes under the sink. This valve controls the flow of water into the line. By comparison, a **gain, trim, attenuation,** or **sensitivity** control at the input of a mixer channel controls the source level into the channel, allowing us to get good pressure without bursting anything. **HA** (**H**ead **A**mp) is another term used by Yamaha, I guess logically because it is a pre*Amp* at the *Head* of the input. You'll see this designation on their digital mixers.

Fader: Note the faucet on top of the sink; this controls the amount you wish to use from the line. So does the channel fader (or volume knob) on a mixer.

Auxes: Now let's say we have an icemaker in the fridge. We hook a small tap and valve off the pipe under the sink and feed the hose over to the icemaker. We've just employed an auxiliary line to feed another device, just as a channel can send to effects or stage monitors. Such channel controls may be called **aux, send, mix** (common on digital mixers), **monitor, effect,** or **foldback** (the last may show up on some older mixers.)

EQ: Finally, we'll hook up an activated charcoal filter on the line to remove impurities from the water. Likewise, the channel **equalizer** section is a filter to control tonal "impurities."

That's all the major channel controls. For each type of level control on each channel, there will be a corresponding overall control in the master section, such as Aux 1 Master, Effect Send Master, L-R/Stereo/Main fader, etc. The whistles will determine our flexibility in choosing how auxes are affected by the other elements on the channel, where we want to route our channel outputs, more EQ control, etc.

INPUT STAGE

Finally, we get back to that part about sources and levels from the start of the book. The proper mixer will provide the balanced and unbalanced input connections needed for your sources. Then the signal goes straight to the *gain* control, where you can accommodate all those great variations in dB levels. You'll bring up the gain control for those low-level mic signals, and bring it down for those hot keyboard signals.

How do you know when the setting is right? Most mixers have a channel peak LED that will light up red when the signal is too hot and might distort or damage something. While the source is playing (or singing) its loudest, bring up the gain until you see peak red. Then drop it back a notch or so and you're set. What if it's all the way down and you still see red? This may occur with hot signals like keyboards and kick drum mics, so some mixers have a gain **PAD** switch (called a **RNGE** switch in the graphic on right) that will drop the level another 10–20dB, giving you more *range* to make your adjustment. A larger mixer may have a four- to eight-LED meter on each channel strip as a better reference for input adjustment. If the mixer has channel **PFL** or **SOLO** switches (see Downtown later in this chapter), they will typically route channel input level to an indicated master meter for more precise display. Then simply adjust gain for a good meter reading. Check the owner's manual for specific details.

There will usually be *phantom power* (or **48V**) switching available somewhere, either as a global switch or near the top individual channels. This cuts on a 24- to 48-volt DC supply to the balanced XLR inputs for those condenser mics we spoke about. The (+) voltage travels down the hot and neutral wire, and the (−) voltage travels through the ground shield. A global phantom power will not bother dynamic mics, but *can be shorted by an unbalanced XLR cable with pin 1 jumped to pin 2 or 3.* (Don't use these!) Phantom power may affect some instrument preamps, including those built into acoustic guitars, but a direct box should eliminate the problem.

Other features can include channel **mute** (on/off) switches, **HPF** (High Pass Filter) switches to reduce bass frequencies, and a *phase reverse* switch (often using the icon ø), which can help if you have a few mics wired up backward, or *out of phase*. I'll talk more about this when we get into some applications. Plus, it's 2 a.m., and I think *my* phase is getting a little reversed.

PRE/POST AUXES

Let's go back to our ice-maker hookup. Tapped off the pipe under the sink, it will obviously be controlled by the input valve. It will not be affected by the faucet, therefore we'll call it a "pre-faucet" tap. If we could hook it up after the faucet, we would call it "post-faucet" tap and it *would* be affected by the faucet. Likewise, if the tap is before the charcoal filter, it is "pre-filter," and impurities will not be removed from the ice-maker line. If it is connected "post-filter," it will get filtered water.

The same goes for channel auxes. They may be tapped off the circuit **pre** or **post EQ**, and **pre** or **post fader**. (The owner's manual should illustrate which ones are which in a basic circuit "map" layout called a **block diagram**.) The better mixers will often include pre/post fader switches, so you'll have a selection for individual or multiple auxes. Pushing the switch activates the labeled mode. Generally speaking, stage monitor feeds are pre-fader auxes. This is so changes you make in channel fader levels for the house balance won't alter monitor levels too, messing up what the performers need to hear or causing mic feedback from variations in monitor levels. However, I often prefer post-fader auxes for many sources in church services since, unlike a typical concert, performers may be changing from week

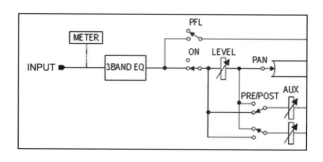

to week. Rather than constantly altering all the pre-fader monitor settings (which may be daunting for volunteer sound people), it can be easier presetting a good monitor balance on each channel that will then adjust appropriately with my house fader moves. This is especially useful for background vocalists. If a particular singer is louder than last week's, I bring them down on the channel fader to balance them in the house and they drop proportionately in the monitors. Or I bring them up a little if it's a softer singer. As a result, balancing their vocals in the house sound simultaneously balances them all in the monitors, too. I've done this for years with all those vocalists being happy with their mix from week to week. (Amazing, huh?)

Post-fader is also preferred for accompaniment soundtracks. If the song is a bit too soft in the beginning, a proper fader increase for the house reflects in the monitors so performers can cue off the music better. If it's a live-performance soundtrack that needs a fade-in or fade-out for start or finish, this will also fade the monitor feed. A pre-fader aux would allow the music to continue blasting through the monitors after the house sound is faded.

To provide flexibility in these instances, it is best when a mixer has pre/post switching on every channel for all auxes, or at least pairs of auxes. This allows me to select the primary vocal leader and instrument channels for pre-fader monitor sends as needed. Though some older mixers had pre-fader auxes that were also *pre-EQ*, it is always better if they are *post-EQ* (the current norm) so that any essential tone adjustment on a vocal or instrument channel will be reflected in the monitors, too. (I'm sure you wouldn't want it to sound great in the house but crappy in the monitors.)

Effects feeds are also post-fader auxes to allow the effects you add to keep balance with the source's fader level. Otherwise, lowering or fading out something like a vocal channel would not proportionately change the level of a reverb effect. However, this can be an interesting effect in the studio where decreasing the voice level while the reverb level stays constant sounds like the voice is disappearing into the distance. If you have a switchable pre-fader aux for a reverb effect, try it sometime when you have a chance.

EQUALIZERS

Many people use EQ like Renuzit air freshener. Something stinks, so they start adding stuff to try to cover it up. You can find these people by looking at their EQ knobs; all the notches will be pointing to the right side. If something stinks in my house, my solution is to get rid of the problem first. (Of course, then I wouldn't have any socks to wear.)

When you're listening to a sound, don't think about what it's missing. Think first about what it's got too much of. This was the basis for my previous drum and wireless-lapel EQ suggestions. If a drum or mic sounds muddy, most people would probably try to cover it up with an abundance of high EQ. This creates frequency peaks that are harsh and prone to feedback. Better to eliminate the muddiness first, then add subtle amounts of high end if needed. In other words, use both sides of the EQ knobs. I typically cut 80 percent of the time to remove the problems. Before we start turning knobs, however, let's find out what we're controlling when we do.

Hertz

Tonal frequencies are designated in Hertz (Hz), or cycles per second. The audible range is 20Hz to 20,000Hz (20kHz, or kilohertz). Below is a graph describing the various frequency ranges along with their positive and negative characteristics. (I hope you appreciate the brilliant terminology.) This should be a valuable aid in learning how to pinpoint and control your equalization.

+	Demolition?	Tight kick	Fullness	Warmth	Definition	Clarity	Brightness	Brilliance
−	Subsonic	Boominess	Muddiness	Hollowness	Harshness	Piercing	Edgy/whistley	Sibilance

L	O	W	M	I	D	H	I	G	H
20Hz	40Hz	70Hz	200Hz	500Hz	2kHz	5kHz	10kHz	20kHz	

From the preceding graph, you can note particular sonic characteristics you need to control and adjust accordingly. Following are some additional tips and information:

50–70Hz: The chest-resonant range where you feel tight kick. Too much is boomy and wastes watts.

100–250Hz: There are usually muddiness problems to take out here, but can also be used to add fullness to a "midrangy" sound.

300–500Hz: Adds warmth to a thin sound. Too much causes a hollow resonance, which can be accentuated by large rooms.

500–2kHz: Critical midrange region for most sources. Cut if sound is harsh or "nasally."

2kHz–5kHz: Guitar edge, drum attack, vocal presence, etc. Ear's most sensitive range, so don't overdo it. Cut if sound is piercing.

5kHz–10kHz: Can add brightness, but too much is prone to a brittle or whistley sound. Electronic hiss is typically above 8kHz.

10kHz–15kHz: Cuts excessive sibilance, or adds sweet-sounding highs on vocals, cymbals, string instruments, etc.

EQ Features

Your stereo hi-fi probably has a bass and treble control. This would be 2-band fixed EQ. The same shows up on the most basic mixers. These are typically *shelving* controls, boosting (to the right) or cutting (to the left) a broad "shelf" of frequencies at 100Hz and below for bass and 10kHz and above for treble. Each notch is a subtle change in the frequency level, and straight up (or 12:00) is flat, or no change. Some units also have a mid control centered at around 1–2.5kHz. It's called a *peak and dip* control because this EQ curve acts as a boosted "hill" or cut "hole" shape centered on the set frequency. So, what if we want to change 500Hz? What if there's *feedback* at 5kHz? We've got a bit of a problem because our midrange control isn't fixed at those points.

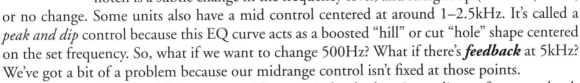

Enter **sweep EQ**. In addition to our midrange gain knob, there is an adjacent frequency knob that allows us to pinpoint a whole range of mid frequencies. Now our midrange isn't limited to a fixed point, but will sweep from say 200Hz to 5kHz. Now I can set it at 5kHz and cut down the mid-gain control to get rid of that feedback. Even if I've got feedback I can't pinpoint, the sweep will help find it. I just set the mid gain at about the 10:00 position and rotate the corresponding frequency knob until I hear the feedback dip or stop. The same can be done for a muddy sound. Rotate frequency until the mud is gone. Then fine adjust the mid gain to take out only as much as you need to. Frequency found. Problem precluded.

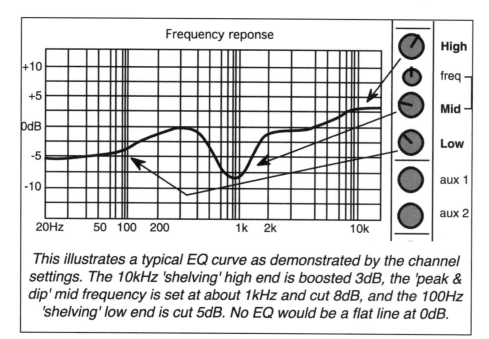

This illustrates a typical EQ curve as demonstrated by the channel settings. The 10kHz 'shelving' high end is boosted 3dB, the 'peak & dip' mid frequency is set at about 1kHz and cut 8dB, and the 100Hz 'shelving' low end is cut 5dB. No EQ would be a flat line at 0dB.

This EQ configuration would be called **3-band with sweep mid**. A better board might have **4-band with dual sweep** (on hi-mid and low-mid controls), or a sweep on all the frequencies. Add a "**Q**" (width) adjustment and you get **parametric EQ** that lets you set how wide a range of frequencies on each side of the midpoint is affected by each sweep. The better the EQ, the more flexibility and ear training you'll get.

One More Tip

Now that you understand something about EQ, it's safe to assume you should start making major adjustments to all your sources, right? *Wrong, bandwidth breath!* A speaker system with accurate response will eliminate the need for excessive tonal adjustments. Sources such as CDs, keyboards, properly miked acoustic instruments, and vocals should require little or no EQ. Some sources that usually require more conscientious adjustment are close-miked drums and piano, instrument pickups run direct, and choir, lapel, and podium mics. Some more techniques will be touched on in Chapter 10.

BUSES & GROUPS

Just as the term seems to imply, **buses** are the lines that transport channels "downtown" to the master section. If there is only one bus line running, you will only have the channel level control for the "bus" downtown. If there are two bus (or stereo) lines, you will also have a channel **pan** control, which can be adjusted to send the channel to the left or right main output or anywhere in between. If there are more than two bus lines, there will be an L-R switch plus additional **assignment switches,** such as 1-2, 3-4, etc., to select which pair(s) you wish to use. (Some mixers may have individual switches for each bus—1, 2, 3, 4, etc.) The pan will again be adjusted to send to the odd- or even-numbered assignment: pan left for 1 or 3, pan right for 2 or 4, and so on. There are typically four or eight assignable buses, and several reasons for them. In recording, it is to

send one or more assigned channels to a multitrack recorder via bus output connections. For example, with eight bus outputs on a mixer, I can connect directly to all inputs of an 8-track studio recorder. Then I can send any mixer channel to any track I want to record on by just assigning to the appropriate bus, 1 through 8.

Another use is **channel grouping,** used more in live applications. It's the reason buses are also called *groups*, and all these groups can be routed to the main outputs. There are many times when it's nice to have a single volume control for a whole bunch of specific channels. In the case of multiple drum mic channels, I can assign them all to Group 1 and then press a switch (usually just above that group's master fader) that routes that group to the L/R output. Then, if I want to control the drum level, I can simply adjust that Group 1 master fader instead of eight channel faders at once. (I wouldn't want to strain myself.) In the same way, I can assign other groups for multiple channels of background vocals, choir, orchestra, rhythm section, etc. If you're using a group assignment switch for a channel, don't forget to unassign the L/R (or Main, Mix, whatever it's called) switch on the channel so it's not going through both a group and the L/R at the same time. That defeats the purpose.

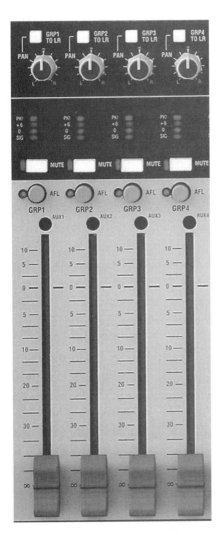

*[Note: Be aware that major live sound mixers utilize **VCA** grouping (or **DCA** grouping in digital mixers), which is different. Though they look like regular group master faders, a **Voltage-Controlled Amplifier** or **Digital-Controlled Amplifier** is actually a sophisticated remote control of the selected channel levels themselves. In this case, you press a channel's VCA/DCA assignment button like normal grouping, but leave the channel L/R switch activated since that is the only switch that actually routes the signal to the main output.]*

DOWNTOWN

In the master section, we'll have a few simple stereo inputs for external effects or playback sources like CD or iPod, master controls for everything routed from the channels, and level meters. Main outputs go to the speaker amplifiers and/or stereo recorders, group outputs can go to a multitrack recorder (if any), and aux outputs can go to effects units, stage and in-ear monitors, or remote sound needs like hallway speakers and wireless hearing-assistance systems. Live sound consoles may also have **Matrix (MTX)** outputs. These are simply "auxes" for master group and L/R buses rather than the channels. They can be used if you wish to send a simpler grouped mix to recorders or those remote sound areas.

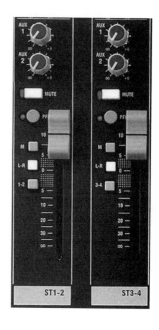

Headphone and **Control Room** (**CR**) outputs on consoles will allow you to monitor the main output as well as any channels or masters via **SOLO** buttons. As the name suggests, SOLO will isolate a selected source to the headphones for your scrutiny. Such buttons may also be called **CUE, PFL** (pre-fader listen), or **AFL** (after-fader listen). The difference is that a PFL signal will allow you to monitor a source with the channel off or fader down so it's not coming through the house, while AFL is affected by the fader and on/off (or mute) switch. If you are soloing multiple background vocals, for instance, AFL will reflect their actual fader balance. PFL is generally used more for live sound to check individual items, and AFL is used in the studio to reference a track's level, EQ, and pan in relation to the overall recording mix. Most larger mixers, including digital, allow you to switch channel or master modes between PFL and AFL.

The extra master inputs I mentioned earlier will be called **Effects** or *Stereo Returns*. They're actually similar to the other channels except that they lack most of the features, like XLR mic inputs, EQ, or auxes. You will need to check specific mixers and their manuals to see what input features they offer in their master package.

Levels: The most important point I can make about levels is not to overdrive your mixer outputs. Your meters will let you know what's going on. Set all your master faders or knobs at *unity gain*, which is usually represented by a "0" or thick mark on most controls. If in doubt, set master faders at two-thirds and knobs at halfway. Adjust individual channel levels as needed. Master meters should hit at 0dB to +3dB maximum for analog mixers. (This can be a little different for digitals, so we'll cover that in the next chapter.) This will guarantee full *clean* output for your mixer. If your system still isn't loud enough for your application, levels for outboard gear like EQs or compressors may be adjusted too low, or your amplifier input levels may need to be increased. If neither, than you simply need *MORE POWER* (amps and speakers that is). You can't solve the problem by overdriving the whole system. More later in Chapter 9, "Power Tools."

RECORDING MIXERS

The things that make recording most different from live sound are the controlled environment, a conceptual approach to the recording process (covered in Chapter 12), and the mixer. While all mixers have essentially the same features, one thing sets recording mixers apart—**track returns**. In live PA, we are dealing with a single-stage process. The sources come into the mixer and are sent out to the speaker system. In multitrack recording, it's a two-stage process. Sources come into the mixer and out to recorder tracks, then back from the recorder to the mixer track returns. These returns are additional channels that allow you to independently monitor tracks during recording or playback while the main channels are being used to send sources to the tracks. Most analog recording consoles are "in-line" designs with dual inputs and controls—for a regular channel and a more basic track return. In other words, two different channels on the same strip! (In the graphic, the track return is called the *MIX-B* section, which only features a pan, mute, and 2-band EQ.) After recording is complete, the special TRACK/CHAN switch "flips" the tracks from the more basic return channel over to the normal feature-packed channel when it is time to mix everything down to stereo.

Another standard feature on a recording mixer is **direct outputs** for each channel on the rear panel, used for sending individual channels directly to recorder tracks (without routing through the master section). There are also separate stereo studio and control room outputs, a talkback mic assignable to studio and tracks, and **2-track** return(s) for playing back the final mix from the stereo deck. (Many of these features are also standard on live sound mixers.)

Occasionally, you could need additional inputs or expanded routing of signals and equipment, or both, especially in the studio. **Patchbays** and **mic preamps** are external devices that can expand on the capabilities of many mixer systems. Though current I/O (Input/Output) capabilities on mixers, especially digital, have rendered patchbays nearly obsolete, I thought you should at least be familiar with their legacy.

Patchbays

As if you didn't have enough connections already, try adding a few hundred more! It could actually provide a convenience in some fixed installations, and you've already gone too far to turn back now. So when there are just too many input and output connections coming from all over a studio or a performance venue and behind your equipment, you can bring them all to one central, accessible spot—the patchbay.

All the desired gear plugs into the back of the patchbay and can be designated with labels (or freehand scribblings for the meticulous) on the front panel. Whenever something needs to be connected to something else, we plug patch cords in the front from designated outputs to designated inputs. There are usually two rows of 16 to 24 connections with a selection of RCA or balanced and unbalanced phone connectors available. A patchbay may also be fixed or switchable for **normaled, half-normaled**, or **non-normaled** operation.

A **normaled** patchbay means it already has internal over/under connections made for you. If, for example, an output like an aux send is hooked to a rear connection on the top row and an effects input is hooked up directly under it, the normaled circuit has already connected them so you don't need a front patch cable from top to bottom. However, if you plug a patch cable into the front jack of either one, it disconnects them so

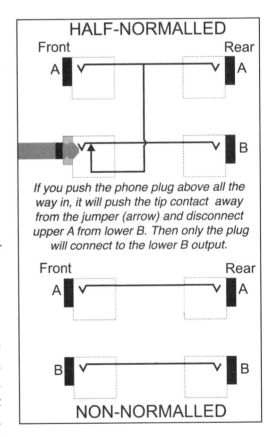

If you push the phone plug above all the way in, it will push the tip contact away from the jumper (arrow) and disconnect upper A from lower B. Then only the plug will connect to the lower B output.

they can be routed elsewhere. (This is a function similar to *insert* jacks on a mixer.) There's also **half-normaled** where only one of the over/under jacks would cause a disconnect (primarily preferred for input connections), and **non-normaled,** where there is no over/under connection. This just makes it possible to expand and tailor a complex system to your specific needs.

Mic Preamps

These units offer basic XLR balanced mic inputs, each with a separate direct output. Simple features include gain, phantom power, some kind of level or peak indication, and maybe phase reverse. No EQ, no auxes, no buses, no downtown. This lack of additional circuitry makes for a high-quality "straightline" design, so they're often used in studio recording for optimal sound straight to the recorder. They're available in solid-state and tube-circuit versions offering one to eight preamps in a single unit.

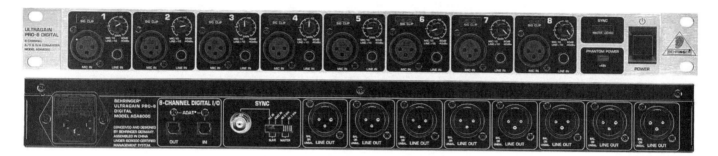

Many preamps now offer internal analog-to-digital conversion for direct digital connection to today's multitracks, workstations, software-based recording systems, and digital mixers. Prices range from $200 for a Behringer ADA8000 (eight XLR inputs and outputs via ADAT digital optical connection) to $2,000 or more for studio models like Universal Audio or Grace Designs. In addition to their studio appeal, they can be useful in live remote recording. Instead of hauling around a large mixer, three rackmount 8-channel mic preamps can provide 24 mic inputs and direct-to-track outputs for 24-track recording in a few spaces of an equipment rack.

PROCESSOR CONNECTIONS

Chapters 8 and 9 are devoted to effects and signal processors, so let's talk about how these are connected to a mixer, either physically or virtually. We'll discuss two types of hookups: **direct** and **sidechain**.

Direct

Signal processors include units such as equalizers, compressors, noise gates, noise reduction, etc. The purpose of these is to process the whole signal to achieve the desired result. One way of doing this is to plug a source straight into a compatible processor and then out of the device to a mixer. Another method is using mixer *inserts*.

Inserts are send and return connections that are available at several points along a mixer's signal path. They will usually be on every channel, allowing signal processors to be easily connected to individual sources. They can also be on groups or main outputs so you can process several things or the whole mix at once.

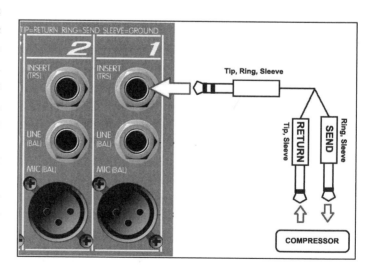

Though some mixers have had separate send and return jacks, most have insert jacks that use a **1/4-inch TRS** phone connection, but not for a balanced function, as you learned for cable input and output connections. Though configuration may vary, the **T**ip is usually the return from the processor, and the **R**ing is the send to it. The **S**leeve is the common ground, as always. When the plug of an **insert cable** is pushed into the insert, it automatically disconnects the channel circuit at that point so the signal has to go through the cable to the processor and back again. The other end of the insert cable has two separate connectors corresponding to the send and return; these plug into the processor input and output respectively. (If you're plugged in with the processor on and you get no sound, you probably just have the two processor connections backward.)

If your mixer manual indicates that the insert jack *Ring* is indeed a send, you can also plug a mono, 1/4-inch phone cable halfway in (just until you feel the first click) to create a pre-fader direct out without the internal jumper of the insert jack disconnecting the channel circuit. This allows you to feed the line-level signal of that insert send to multichannel recording or monitoring systems without affecting the normal channel operation.

Side-Chain

Unlike a signal processor, an effect such as reverb or echo is an embellishment to the original signal. It doesn't need to process the whole signal, just be added to it. Accordingly, it is normally connected to an *aux* output, which sends its "side" signal to the effect input, and then the effect output is patched to an *effects return* to be added to the mix. Since all channels have routing to the aux outputs, the side-chained effect can be added to any or all of those channels. Also, a regular channel can be used as an effects return if you need the added features of EQ, pan, or monitor and recording sends for the effect. Just don't loop an

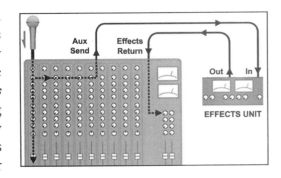

effect through itself by inadvertently bringing up the aux send on its own return channel. Otherwise, you'll get a loud squeal equivalent to a nerve-racking aria from a bad soprano.

Another point is that effects units have a **balance** or **mix** control. This determines how much original signal is mixed in with the effect. In a mixer side-chain hookup, we already have original signal passing straight through the mixer, so we don't want it added from the effects unit again. So set the effect's mix control all the way to "wet," "effect," 100 percent, whatever your unit calls it. (That terminology thing, again.) If you choose to run a source direct through an effects unit or patched through an insert connection, this is not side-chain, so you'll need to adjust the mix control for the desired blend of original signal and effect.

Now, take everything you've just learned about mixer features and multiply it exponentially, throw in an extensive virtual patchbay system, add all the effects and signal processing you'll learn about in coming chapters, digitize everything in software and put it in a fancy-looking package, give it a memory and a mind of its own (whoa, we're getting scary now!), and you'll have the wonder of . . . *(yeah, this means turn the page)*

Virtual Plumbing 201

6

AN INTRODUCTION

Well, hasn't digital technology just blown wide open! In addition to the boom in internet and handheld communications technology, digital mixers and recorders have made affordable world-class performance and features available to the masses. What gives digital products this potential for superiority? Let me offer a simple illustration:

An architect in Virginia prepares artwork of a house for a fellow architect in California. Once finished, he makes a copy of his final draft and sends a fax of it to his associate. As you can imagine, with old fax technology, significant quality and detail will be lost in the transition by attempting to pass the original through this "analog" process.

On the other hand, let's say the same architect opts to print an extensive list of instructions describing exact dimensions, angles, features, Pantone colors, etc. of the drawing. He makes a copy and again sends a fax. Even if it's only barely readable, his associate can redraw a perfect version from the instructions. This is the "digital" process.

In digital audio, the sound is turned into digital instructions (1s and 0s) by an **analog-to-digital (AD) converter**. When it's ready to be retrieved for analog reproduction (such as with amps and speakers), the digital info is perfectly "redrawn" to analog form by a **digital-to-analog (DA) converter**. Result: a beautiful picture! When we record, we use this basic process as a means to simply store the original picture for later listening, transferring, or editing. With mixers and other audio equipment, however, converting to digital gives us a unique environment for accurately and efficiently manipulating the picture in almost any way imaginable.

Digital Domains: The thing that never ceases to amaze me is that the sounds we hear can be represented by a single waveform (or two for stereo). And from that waveform, which a speaker or headphone reproduces with sound pressure changes as it moves back and forth, our magical ears can distinguish anything from a solo acoustic guitar to the collective sounds of a 60-piece orchestra. It is this complex waveform that the mixing or recording process must capture accurately.

In the digital domain, we can see this waveform picture as a graph. The vertical graduations are represented by the **bit resolution**. The term *16-bit* means we have 16 numbers to designate and two possibilities for each number, a 1 or a 0. The total number of possibilities are 216 or 65,536. The horizontal graduations are represented by the **sampling rate**, usually 48k (48,000 times per second). So for each 1/48,000th of a second, we can put a dot on one of over 65,000 vertical points to plot our waveform—pretty fine detail if you ask me. And if we go to 20-bit technology, we'll have 220, or over 1,000,000, vertical points to choose from! This

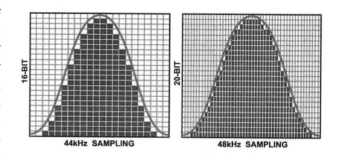

means an even smoother drawing with more dynamic range, which is the amount of "vertical" headroom we have available for level from our softest to loudest passages. All in all, the higher the resolution, the clearer and more accurate the reproduction. Currently, we've seen digital audio get to 32-bit/96k sampling and some processing to 56-bit!

Why am I telling you all this? So you'll have a little better understanding of the technology that has permeated every aspect of audio—mixers, recorders, effects, and signal processors. Who could have imagined a decade ago that today you could have the capabilities of a $100,000 analog theatre console in a $2,500 digital mixer, or a complete digital multitrack recording and mixing system for less than that? (Nostradamus said nothing about it.) In addition, digital allows the implementation of internal, software-based audio components that duplicate sophisticated external units costing thousands of dollars, putting complete audio systems in one package and eliminating associated cable integration, which can add to noise and sound degradation.

The first time I started using a digital mixer in a studio after a decade on analog, I found myself still unconsciously bound to engineering techniques based around the limitations of analog. Suddenly I stopped, pushed myself away from the console, and sat a bit stunned realizing that I now had unlimited potential sitting in front of me. I was going to have to consciously clear my mind of all the self-imposed confinements of past technology and let my imagination soar. That is the first step in using digital mixers to their full potential.

For the same reasons computer-based video systems have replaced overhead and slide projectors, digital mixers now bless us with capabilities inconceivable with analog systems. Yamaha was the first to introduce affordable digital mixers, like the Promix 01, 02R, and 03D, in the mid-'90s, establishing this new precedent in mixing technology. These were followed several years later by offerings from Tascam, Mackie, and a few others. By 2005, most manufacturers had started jumping on the digital bandwagon with varying success. Consequently, most of the die-hard analog users finally realized they were going to have to adapt to this new world. If you're new to sound and digital mixing, anything less will seem like the Stone Age.

Since you've just been through a mixer primer, I'll proceed into sections that echo those of the last chapter so we can cover the expanded features inherent to digital mixers. While most digital mixers had initially been designed with a combination of live and recording use in mind, we have witnessed a definite split to more specific models for live sound. Though my graphics will represent a variety of mixers, I'll

base much of my discussion on Yamaha mixer features and terminology since the variations throughout the market can be endless. Though these may differ slightly from products offered by other companies, the primary functions are the same and it is reasonable to assume that you may run into more Yamaha mixers due to their proliferation. They also set some standards for this new digital realm, beating the others on the technology by at least a decade (almost unprecedented in audio innovation), and they're still on the cutting edge of product releases. I'm pleased to give them some well-deserved recognition because they were the first to make my audio life a whole lot easier.

EVERYTHING AND THE COMPUTER LINK

Digital mixers have all the same basic elements as analog, plus a lot more, as you'll soon learn. But you will notice that digital mixers don't have as many knobs as analogs. For one thing, this keeps the size manageable since a digital could have at least three times the knobs for all the added features. (Think about that if you ever see an older Yamaha 48-channel PM5000 analog and your head will spin.) It also keeps price down by avoiding literally hundreds of costly software-controlling encoders on the mixer surface.

Instead, digitals offer a combination of faders and knobs that can serve multiple functions, Pick a channel using its **SEL**ect button, and its vast array of controls are in a **SELECTED CHANNEL** area on the surface of the mixer and also duplicated in dedicated function screens in the display. One distinct advantage here is that the clueless don't have as many knobs to fiddle with, while the competent are encouraged to know more about the ones they do. That can mean better results for everyone.

Faders

Digitals save cost and space with motorized faders and fader layers. A mixer may have only 16 channel faders, but can have 32 actual channels available. A button somewhere will select channels 1–16 (on the first layer) or 17–32 (on a second layer). Some larger digitals may have 24 faders and

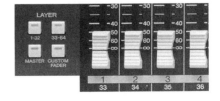

a third or fourth layer for up to 96 channels. Since the faders are motorized and digitally remember their settings, you will see them move to the settings for each layer you select. Any adjustments you make affect only the selected layer, and any of those changes will be retained as you switch through other layers.

In live sound, I prefer to have all my primary channels available on the first layer. In the spontaneity of the moment, you can lose track of which layer you're on, so live digitals are incorporating more faders for minimizing channel fader layers, though they will always have other layers for various send and master faders. We'll cover some other features of motorized faders in the next few sections.

Thanks for the Memory

As I said, the fader settings on a particular layer are retained as you move through other layers, and most mixers will remember your most current adjustments even if you lose power or switch the unit off. But to revert from this temporary buffer memory to permanent memory, you need to store the settings in **Scene memory**. This is a menu of numerous memory locations for naming, storing, protecting, and recalling complete mixer configurations, including all your levels, aux settings, EQ, panning, processing, routing, and external digital interfacing and control parameters.

In the recording studio, I can have different scenes for different songs, sections of a song, or even varied mixes of those songs. For a church sound system, I can have scenes stored for various services, rehearsals, concerts, weddings, day-school programs, etc. Even if someone has messed with all my controls, I can press one or two buttons and everything is perfectly reset and ready to go. A teacher who knows absolutely nothing about mixers can be trained to push those same buttons and activate a perfect sound setup for her kids' preschool rehearsal. You can't beat that for convenience and consistency. There are also individual memories for EQ, compression, routing, and more, which I'll talk about in their respective sections.

INPUT STAGE

All the standard mixer input connections available, all with that AD (analog-to-digital) conversion inside. Once the analog input signal is converted, it can remain digital for the rest of its journey until it has to output through amps and speaker systems. Inputs still have a *gain* control, *phantom power* (48V) on XLR inputs, and possibly a **pad** or *phase reverse* (ø) switch, typically the only nondigital circuits prior to conversion, though most consoles now incorporate digital control of these items so they can be memorized with the other parameters. There may also be channel *inserts* on the rear panel so external analog processing can be patched into the predigital circuit. From that point on, all is software-based and can therefore be stored in memory.

PRE/POST AUXES

(Note: SENDS has become the more common term for channel auxes on digital boards, so I will predominantly use that in this section.)

All limitations disappear here. Even smaller mixers usually have at least eight **sends** (also called **mixes**), all with individual pre/post switches for each channel, plus flexible routing to any output connector or any effects units built into the mixer. This means you can have a send routed to any of 4 to 24 standard output connectors (depending on mixer model), and you can even route a single send to multiples of these outputs if you need the same mix to several destinations. All of the above are available in a specified SEND

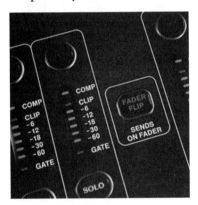

(or MIX) control section on the mixer surface as well as on related pages in the digital display. Their routing control is typically found on input/output PATCH or I/O pages.

You also have the capability of controlling send levels with the channel faders. The advantage of faders is easier access and control (try controlling multiple knobs at the same time) and a better visual reference of those channel levels. Imagine if we had enough funds and real estate to equip an analog mixer with faders for all its sends as well—we'd need a boom lift to get around the board! With digital, two things make this control capability feasible: **motorized faders** that move to preset positions, and **fader layers** that can activate different banks of level control.

A feature often termed *SENDS-ON-FADER* mode allows you to select any of your send switches (such as Mix1 or Mix16 on a Yamaha), and then your channel faders turn into send levels for each channel, making it much easier to see at a glance where all the levels are set. No more hunting for a row of aux knobs on an analog channel or trying to see where each is set. If you wish to bring up piano on the lead singer's Mix1 stage monitor, press the Mix1 select button (may also be a push-knob), you'll see all the faders switch to that layer, and bring up the piano channel fader. Only it's not a channel anymore; it's a send! Simple once you get used to it. When you're finished with adjustments, press another button and you're back to the main channel's fader layer.

(Note: Sends-On-Fader is normally provided as an option to using dedicated send knobs in the SEND/MIX control section of the mixer. But for consoles with no such dedicated send controls, it is the primary way to adjust send levels short of using their on-screen page.)

There are a few other ways to control send levels on most mixers. After the sound check and when I'm into a live performance, I prefer to keep faders in the channel level mode for house control and adjust monitors as needed through separate dedicated controls. The SEND section is the easiest way with dedicated control of the send level. There are also SEND or CHANNEL on-screen pages. These pages display send level, on/off, and pre/post settings for the selected channel that can be adjusted by touchscreen, or by a row of "soft knob" encoders under the screen (so-called because their function changes according to adjacent on-screen designations), or with a data wheel and navigating cursor buttons on the mixer surface. Some mixers may also have a special encoder knob available just above the channel fader that is switchable for controlling a selected send as well as other channel functions. All this means is that you have a few ways to make adjustments that suit your own engineering style or situation. As with any mixer, your preferred methods will soon become second nature.

EQUALIZERS

On previous analog mixers, we were fortunate to have **4-band with dual-sweep EQ** available without breaking the bank. But we're more fortunate to have **4-band, full-parametric EQ** on digitals that puts those to shame. To solidify the point, where the former offered 6 knobs of control, the latter offers 12. And digital EQ is much more precise. I first discovered this when the parametric EQ in a small digital board outperformed a high-end analog 31-band graphic EQ for tuning subwoofers. As a result, I started eliminating analog graphic EQs.

Digitals typically have a single set of dedicated EQ knobs (again in its Selected Channel area), and you simply select a channel to make the adjustments. Some analog engineers might claim this is more complicated, but it's really not. Both are a three-stage process. With analog, you (1) move to the channel, (2) move up the strip to the specific EQ control, and (3) turn the knob. With digital, you (1) press the channel's SELect or EDIT button, (2) move to the dedicated EQ band in the Selected Channel section (sometimes this means pressing a band button), and (3) turn the knob.

A couple things that make digital more efficient are that one hand can remain in the same EQ area while you select different channels for adjustment, and you can see more precise EQ parameters and even the EQ curve itself in the mixer's display. Did you ever wonder what frequency that analog sweep knob was on when it was at 2:30? Now the digital tells you it's exactly at 3.55kHz. As you hear that change and see the curve, you're actually getting advanced ear training for free!

Digitals don't have parametric EQ only on the input channels—they normally have it on all the outputs as well, allowing you to fine-tune mains and monitors or your overall recording mix. I often find that they give me as much precise control as I require. With good speakers and a room of moderate size, there are normally only three or four problem areas. But these days, most mixers also incorporate internal graphic EQs that can be patched to any channel or output. Now you have graphics with digital precision that you can use for your main and monitor outputs or insert into channels when needed. (We'll discuss graphics and other signal processors in Chapter 8, "Signal Corps.")

Now the convenience of individual memory functions starts. Any specific EQ adjustments you set for a channel or output can be stored in an **EQ library**. There is a link for these libraries on most pages that involve processing and patching EQ, compression, input/output connections, etc. The link will take you to a menu where you can name, store, and recall various settings, usually with at least 100 memory locations to choose from. It may be a dedicated library page for a specific item such as EQ, or one main library page with multiple tabs for accessing any of the various memories.

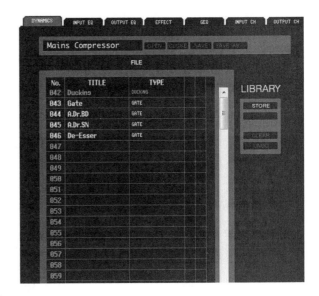

I may use 16 matching wireless headworn mic systems for a theatre production and wish to start with a useful EQ setting for all of them. I can set that EQ on one of the channels, select and store it into the library as "Headworn," and then recall (or copy) that title setting on every channel with a couple of speedy button pushes each. This last step would take about five seconds total. (Try that with manual knobs!) Or I can move a mic or instrument to another channel and recall its EQ instantly.

But wait . . . there's another library I prefer for that. With Yamaha, it's called an **Input** or **Channel library**. (Other brands may offer something similar in their libraries.) This library stores all the channel's parameters at once, including EQ, channel and send levels, pans, compressor settings (which we'll get into shortly) . . . you name it. Now, if I have similar channel sources or move a source to another channel, I'll use the Input library to transfer all the settings at once instead of having to recall them from individual libraries.

After I've set up all the channels on my mixer, my standard backup procedure is to go through available channel library memories, naming and storing each consecutive channel in order. This gives me a "safety" of each individual channel named by source and numbered for its proper place in case I ever have to quickly restore a channel or use it for another similar item as a good starting point. And though I've never had a Yamaha digital mixer fail in over 20 years of use, I still back up all of the mixer's memory data via computer software, smartcard, and/or direct thumbdrive port. With rental companies now stocking the more popular models, I may well be able to rent a replacement in a day or two if my mixer fails (or buy one used and *cheap* on eBay!), make all the connections, and load the memory in a minute or two. Then I'm back in business as if nothing happened.

BUSES & GROUPS

Digital mixers geared more toward recording applications will have the same eight buses for channel assignments found on larger analog mixers, and *pan* controls will still select left/right and odd/even outputs. The eight buses can again be used to send signals to a multitrack recorder or other destinations, and the digital will give you options on routing to analog or digital bus output connections on the mixer that you wish to use. (We'll cover those shortly in the I/O Options section.) For *groups*, however, the larger live-sound digitals incorporate physical DCA faders, which I mentioned along with VCAs in the previous chapter. DCAs

(Digital-Controlled Amplifiers) again serve as assignable remote controls for groups of channel levels. There can be eight or more DCAs depending on the mixer.

What if your digital doesn't have DCA faders? Then it will likely offer an alternative feature. Yamaha consoles have offered **fader-linking,** where the motorized faders can be physically linked by selecting multiple channels to a fader group. Then, when you move any channel fader in the group, all the others magically follow it. Now *any* of those faders serves as a remote control for all the others. With four to eight linking groups available, I can fader-group my background vocals, choir, drums, and orchestra independently.

Okay, you smart guys might be saying, "What if I've set different levels for the various linked channels? If they all physically come down together, won't the lowest ones cut off first?" Initially, I would commend you for being perceptive enough to consider their relative levels. Then I would explain that fader-linking in digital mixers is "intelligently" scaled. If you have this linking feature available, set the channel levels at widely varying positions, link all the faders, and then slowly bring them down (using one fader, of course). You will see that the faders change relative physical position to maintain relative levels, and they all reach bottom at the same time! Yes, the digital designers were way ahead of you.

Linking may also provide a more comprehensive **Channel Link,** which allows you to select numerous parameters to be linked for multiple channels. If I have four choir mics and I want changes in their EQs, send levels, and channel on/off to always be identical, I can link the EQ, SENDs, and CH ON for all four mics. Then any of these changes I make to one, even spontaneously, will automatically be duplicated on all the others. Remember when I talked about realizing the potential at the beginning of this chapter? Hey, we're only just getting started!

DOWNTOWN

The Downtown area will include some of the basic features we have on analog, including extra stereo inputs, and the main L/R faders. To save space, other master level faders for aux, matrix, and group buses (if they aren't provided as dedicated DCA faders) will typically be in a Master fader layer and/or in display pages. Central to the master area is the display screen that provides comprehensive graphics and information within numerous function-specific pages. As mentioned previously, this display will provide touchscreen, soft-button, and/or cursor and data wheel control for accessing and adjusting parameters on-screen.

Many digital mixers also offer a free computer software download (like Studio Manager for Yamaha or X32-Edit for Behringer) with extensive display and control for real-time or offline editing of settings and memories, all communicated via USB or Ethernet connections on the mixer. I've used this software offline at home, relaxing with my laptop, to preset a mixer according to an

artist's tech rider for a pending concert. (I'll explain more about riders later in this chapter.) On the day of the concert, I simply upload these preliminary settings in a few seconds and have all that work done before the sound check. Of course, most newer mixers also offer simpler smartphone and tablet apps for controlling some primary functions like mix and monitor levels, though it's only a fraction of what the computer programs offer.

Where very few analog mixers have a full meter bridge showing levels for all channels and outputs, even the smallest digitals have HOME or METER pages that display any number of comprehensive meters for checking levels at any input or output, and you can select either pre- or post-fader points for indication. With pre-fader, you can check a channel input gain or make sure a channel is active before you bring up the fader. With post-fader, you can balance background vocalists or other sources visually by setting their respective faders so the meter levels are all relatively even. (Useful if the engineer has a tin ear.) Or you can quickly notice which of eight mics that guy is actually talking on so you can adjust the right one.

Like analogs, digitals have a talkback feature (assignable to pretty much any output on the board) and a headphone output to monitor points along the audio path. Recording models will also have studio/control room outputs as well as digital and analog 2-track inputs for simple playback from recording decks or other stereo sources. Solo buttons again let you monitor one or more channels through the headphones or control room speakers, and you have a switchable choice of PFL or AFL soloing for most channels and outputs.

Usually you won't see external ***effects returns*** but rather additional stereo line or return channels specifically routable from internal effects, just as sends and inserts are internally routable to those effects. And unlike analogs, the return channels on digitals will normally have all the same features as regular channels, including 4-band, full-parametric EQ, access to all aux sends, and flexible routing.

PROCESSORS

Now we have to break a little from the format of the last chapter to cover unique extras in the digital environment. One of the greatest luxuries is an abundance of sophisticated signal processing, giving unprecedented control and eliminating the need for most external devices covered in the next two chapters. For example, there can be anywhere from two to eight internal multi-effects units that can be digitally "patched" to any send or channel insert. These will provide everything from reverbs and delays to pitch shift and electric guitar effects.

Even more amazing is the inclusion of compressor/limiters on every channel and output. This can protect the whole system from excessive levels, maintain maximum desired levels for your recording or house sound, or automatically limit and balance sources such as background vocals. (At the end of this chapter, I'll give you a few tips for compressor settings that will get you started in these areas.)

Though digitals have parametric EQ on the outputs, larger live sound models currently include up to 16 graphic EQs that can be patched wherever needed. Along with all the other effects and signal processing, any settings and routing can be stored in libraries and scene memories to be recalled with your normal performance setups.

I/O OPTIONS

A smaller mixer may come standard with 16 input and 6 output connectors, but has 32 channels inside, eight auxes, and a potential for up to 22 outputs! What's wrong with this picture? Nothing's wrong, you're just experiencing *open architecture*. This allows flexibility for expansion while keeping the basic system economical (you may only need 16 channels). Open architecture means we can add on a selection and quantity of connections

that serve our particular purpose, sometimes in the form of option card slots. If we need ADAT digital connections for external mic preamps or recording gear, we can add them. If we need eight more line inputs for wireless mics and eight more outputs for stage monitors, we can add them. If we need 16 feeds to CAT5 output for an Aviom digital in-ear monitor mix system, we can add them.

An earlier design Yamaha MY16AT plug-in card added up to 16 digital inputs and outputs using the **ADAT** optical multichannel format. A

DM2000 mixer I used had six slots for these 16x16 cards, allowing expansion of the 24-channel/10-output mixer to 96 inputs and outputs by interfacing with Behringer ADA8000 preamps. Those inputs then went to additional channels already available in the mixer, and the extra outputs could be routed for almost anything from monitor mixes to multitrack recorders.

MOD POD

Many digital mixers come self-contained, including all the necessary **I/O** (**I**nput/**O**utput) connections on the rear panel just like an analog console. But it has become standard to offer some version of enhanced connectivity that may utilize special card slots, Ethernet, or proprietary connections for a digital snake and remote I/O modules, or to provide compatibility with other audio gear and formats.

Modular designs for live sound provide another approach to flexibility for building a system. A modular design means the actual mixer with all its electronics and input/output connections is in a rackmount box located at the stage (like an oversized, powered snake box). Most of the inputs and outputs will plug straight into that mixer box, eliminating the need for costly and bulky multichannel snakes integrating all those lines to the engineer's console. Then the component that actually looks like the mixer with all the faders and knobs is, for the most part, a big remote control surface with a digital link to the mixer box. (A few essential inputs and outputs will still be provided on the console to handle stereo playback sources, booth monitors, etc.) If you need more channels, you can simply add another box cascaded from the first, and the console will accommodate the extra I/O without requiring additional cabling to the sound booth. Some models also allow you to parallel the digital connect to a second console for stage monitor control, again remotely controlling all the sends in the mixer box itself without complex, isolated audio splits. And with digital control instead of audio lines running through the integrating "snake," there is no loss of quality from hundreds of feet of cable.

This technology became a reality with the first Yamaha PM1D digital modular console used for major events and broadcasts around the world, and now other companies like Avid, Soundcraft, and Allen Heath are offering modular designs in their product lines. Thankfully, the prices have also come down from the PM1D's initial $100,000+ price tag, so I don't need to have a defibrillator handy when I present my next mixer recommendation to the church budget committee.

We're now seeing the development of ever simpler and more powerful audio networking formats, like **Dante** by Audinate, which are being incorporated into digital mixer systems. Dante, like others, uses standard Ethernet cabling to control expansion of up to 64 inputs and 64 outputs. The problem with something like the ADAT optical Toslink cables is that they are limited to less than 50 feet. Ethernet offers broader compatibility, can travel hundreds of feet, and you can even construct the cables yourself using tools and parts from local suppliers.

A late variation on the theme is a mixer box with no control surface; an iPad or other tablet becomes the *whole* mixing console using a free downloaded app. Behringer, Mackie, and PreSonus are a few to break into this new domain with 16- to 32-channel models, and they are incorporating their own Wi-Fi into the units so you aren't at the mercy of available and dependable networks in the area—especially if it's a bluegrass concert on a mountain in the middle of nowhere! There are also standard features like MIDI and Ethernet connectivity, and 8 to 18 outputs available. Another creative and economical option in digital mixing.

OTHER FEATURES

Patching

Just as we used analog patchbays for flexible I/O patching of external components, digitals offer virtual patchbays for making all internal input, output, and processor connections. In PATCH or I/O pages, any input can be routed to any channel. Now you can avoid a rat's nest of cable swapping behind the board to keep various sources like drums, vocals, keyboards, and guitars grouped together on your mixer channels, even though they come from lines all over the stage. Just plug stage lines 1–32 into inputs 1–32 and then virtually route them to any channel you want. If a guitarist moves to the other side of the stage, just repatch that stage line to the same channel so you won't have to transfer all those settings to a different channel.

In the same manner, you can patch mixer outputs to any available output connectors: direct outs from channels (selectable pre- or post-fader), aux sends, bus or main stereo outputs, and even insert sends. This includes patching to any I/O cards or external interfacing integral or added to the system. And numerous patch setups can be stored in libraries so you can change the whole configuration in an instant and save it with scene memories. This patch memory may also include a naming function so you can personally name each input and output for on-screen display to help keep track of what's what. Some boards have fluorescent or LCD name displays above each channel and output fader, which conveniently replace handmade labels and can change with each scene memory.

Recording Mixers

With all this I/O expansion and patching, just about any digital can serve a dual purpose as a live or recording mixer. Rather than requiring an in-line, dual-input design like earlier analog recording consoles, a digital allows the flexible input patching to route sources to any channels and out to a multitrack recorder (using buses or direct outs), and then feeding recorder track returns to other fader layers for monitoring and mixdown.

Rather than employing a dual-input "flip" switch, the fader layers can accommodate multiple recording and mixdown configurations as needed for your production process. And unlike the basic "track return" input of analogs, which had limited features, all digital channels are full-featured so you have optimum processing for both sources and tracks, including storing your mix settings as you add tracks and progress through the project. With a DM2000 96-channel studio console, I used channels 1–48 (fader layers 1 and 2) for the inputs from stage, used their pre-fader direct outs routed to my multitrack recorder, and brought the track returns back into channels 49–96 (fader layers 3 and 4). I only needed to listen to 49–96 to monitor the tracks feeding through the multitrack during recording and then to mix down after all tracks were laid.

Recording consoles may also include a version of Automix (another Yamaha term), a memory function that receives timecode from an audio recorder and remembers adjustments you make to the mix while the recorder (and its timecode) is running. With multitrack mixdown, you can work on one channel at a time—fader moves, on/off switches, pans, EQ changes, effects, etc.—building your mix while the board memorizes each move you make. When you're finished, push a button and it automatically plays back your entire perfected mix in sync with the timecode. For me, this eliminated our days of AMD (Analog Mixdown Disorder) when three people with six hands and caffeine overdose made all-night attempts to manually get a big mix right for the umpteenth time!

External Control

In years past, having control of monitor mixes onstage meant either having the main mixer onstage or incorporating an expensive split-snake of all the stage lines—one to the house board and the other to a separate monitor board. With the advent of digital mixers, the first technology to provide remote control was **MIDI** (**M**usical **I**nstrument **D**igital **I**nterface). MIDI is more popular as a control format for keyboards and sequencers, but it's also a common feature on digital mixers for remote control of external MIDI gear or vice-versa. So you can actually remote-control any digital mixer using a separate MIDI controller, digital workstation (an all-in-one digital mixer/recorder), or another digital mixer large or small.

Though MIDI has a 5-pin plug, it only uses three pins for standard functions. So two XLR-to-MIDI adapters can be easily constructed that allow a MIDI connection through a standard mic cable, and despite what the experts say, I've had no problem with such basic control through a single mic line in a 200-foot audio snake.

(Note: I have a YouTube video tutorial showing how to implement MIDI control for adjusting a stereo recording or broadcast mix of a main house mixer from a remote location. You can find it by searching "MIDI Remote Control video" or by using the URL www.youtube.com/watch?v=fptHiP1lzM4.)

Once receiving the MIDI output of the remote control unit, I could access the main mixer's Control Change page to set what parameters the remote unit controls, which can include any fader levels, send levels, EQ, pan, on/off, etc. My choice was to control a stereo-paired send for video streaming and recording. Since the main mixer's send levels are on a separate fader layer, I could be doing all kinds of fader adjustments for the video mix, and the house engineer would have no idea what's transpiring in the "virtual background."

Though such genius innovation on my part may have served a specific need, current digital technology offers a variety of amazing control resources, including the free management software for computers, smartphones, and tablets I spoke of earlier. Now it is possible to adjust the house mixer through a wireless Wi-Fi network from any seat in the house. Or a touring engineer can walk in with a thumbdrive on his key ring that will plug into a digital mixer and download all his presets in an instant for a major concert. Despite it all, if you occasionally take some time to just sit and ruminate "out of the box" on what might be possible with all that unbridled technology, you could well come up with some innovative genius of you own.

DIGITAL TIPS

One of the most important steps with a digital mixer, particularly in live applications, is initial setup, which includes proper routing of inputs and outputs, adjusting the system for proper gain structure throughout, tuning internal graphic EQs for mains and monitors, and setting compressors on master outputs for protection and controlling levels. I believe these should be performed by the installer or another specialist because it will ultimately determine the overall performance of the system from then on. Once set, these crucial parameters can then be stored and carried over to just about every created scene, so a majority of the setup work will already be done. I accomplish this by storing a "BASIC" scene #1 which may also include a good soundcheck and setup of normal channels used for services or events. This scene will then be protected so it can't be altered. (I usually store another copy of it at the far end of the scene memory as a "hidden" backup in case someone does unprotect and corrupt scene #1.)

When I want to create a scene for a particular event, I simply start with this BASIC scene, copy it to another location, and begin the process of adjusting and storing the setup for that event. That way I always have that optimal and consistent starting point to work from for every event I create.

Levels

All the digitals I've used have a pretty hot output. You may notice that analog mixer meters have a "0dB" **unity gain** indication about two-thirds up the meter with 6dB or a bit more above that for some extra headroom. The 0dB represents the optimal +4dB output level of your mixer (also indicated in the equipment specifications). Digital mixers, especially those for recording, usually indicate 0dB at the top of the meter since –20dB became a standard for *unity gain* for digital audio meters. Therefore, a full "0" reading on your digital meter exiting a +4dB output connector could mean an actual +24dB (4dB + 20dB) heading to your amps. So to maintain better gain for the whole sound system, average peak levels on full-0 digital meters should run around –12dB, giving you at least 12dB of headroom before the mixer peaks out. If your digital does designate 0dB about two-thirds of the way up the meters, run it 0db to +3dB like a normal analog. Your internal compressor settings will help keep the rest under control.

For recording via digital coaxial, optical, or AES/EBU connections, metering is slightly different. Digital multitrack and stereo recorders want full level and resolution, so getting close to full 0dB meter levels from the mixer (avoiding peaks) will deliver optimal levels for your recording equipment. You'll also notice that the recorder input meter levels will be identical.

Once you have this proper level set for all master outputs with your loudest program material running, just set your amplifier input levels for the maximum comfortable volume you desire in the room. Don't run amp levels full up unless you actually need that much volume. (More in Chapter 9, "Power Tools.") Just to be safe, digital manufacturers often allow a little headroom above peak on their meters to avoid distortion, but unfortunately, you won't know how much headroom they have allowed for. So you'll need to make sure you stay below the peak to ensure you're in a safe zone.

I run the individual channels closer to their full levels in multitrack recording for maximum digital *resolution* from each channel (that smooth waveform I talked about in the beginning), but in live sound, most of my individual channels run in the –12dB to –6dB range for dynamic headroom, and so they maintain a

proper combined level through the main outputs. Though input gains are the primary adjustment, there are some unique features for controlling channel levels, including other potential gain controls: an **ATT/Attenuator** (in CHANNEL or EQ displays) or a compressor **Output Level** (in DYNAMICS displays).

If I have analog input gain knobs that are not memorized with scenes (these will be on external preamps or some earlier digital mixers), I may choose to set as many of those gains as possible at an equal level (maybe 10:00) that will not peak out with the hottest sources. Otherwise, I will need to constantly alter those non-memorized settings whenever I patch in different sources from the stage, which is counter to the consistency of digital recall. With a good uniform setting, those analog gains could be compatible with just about anything I plug in. Then I can use an internal digital attenuator and maybe compressor output to fine-tune for specific channels, and these can be stored in scenes and channel libraries. If a podium mic needs more level for distance pickup, I could bring up its internal gains. If I need less level for a hot keyboard signal, I could drop those gains. The range of some of these internal level adjustments can be as much as ±18dB, allowing for more flexibility in how you can control and memorize your level setups.

Since master outputs are blessed with the same attenuation and compression controls, I can also use them for some "safety" functions. For instance, instead of storing a lower main fader setting for a more reserved program (yes, maybe due to some volume complaints), I can set my stereo output fader at full level and store its "hidden" internal attenuator at a lower level so sound volunteers aren't accidentally (or intentionally) cranking up the main fader to uncomfortable levels or feedback. In multitrack mixdown, if I've finished recording all my fader moves in Automix but find a channel or master level is a bit too high or low, I can quickly adjust and store an internal gain for that item without re-recording Automix fader moves.

Channels

Like an analog mixer, the channels should be arranged in a manner that is easily managed, keeping similar sources together in physical groups so you aren't hunting all over the place for the various voices and instruments, especially in live applications. Don't be tempted to change the logical order of channels for every scene or service just because it's possible with the touch of a button. Everyone on the board should use a common layout so they automatically know where everything is no matter who's engineering.

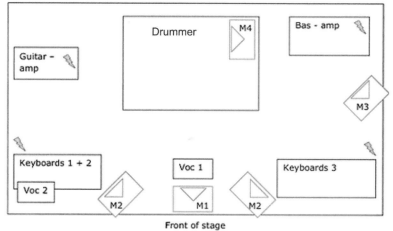

Front of stage

Ch.	Instrument	Mic/DI*	48v	Insert	Notes
1	BD	B52/B91/D112		Gate 1	
2	SD1	SM57			
3	SD2	SM57			
4	HH	Condenser	x		
5	Tom 1	Beta 98		Gate 2	
6	Tom 2 (gulv)	Beta 98		Gate 3	
7	OH L	SM 94/Cond	x		
8	OH R	SM 94/Cond	x		
9	Bas	DI			
10	El-guitar	SM57			
11	Keyboards 1L	DI			
12	Keyboards 1R	DI			
13	Keyboard 2 (mono)	DI			
14	Keyboards 3 L	DI			
15	Keyboards 3 R	DI			
16	Voc 1	SM58		Comp 1	
17	Voc 2	OM5/SM58		Comp 2	

Major artists provide concert riders for the tech needs of their live performances, and most include a pretty standard channel layout for ease of operation by any engineer. For anything from rock concerts to worship events (whether an analog or digital board), a typical layout starting from channel #1 at the left of the mixer follows this order: drum mics, bass, guitars (or other stringed instruments), keyboards, orchestra or solo instruments (violin, sax, etc.), choir or ensemble, background vocals, lead vocals, speaking mics (host, pastors, etc.), and playback sources (CD, iPod, DVD, computer media, etc.). Drum mics can be arranged kick, snare, hi-hat, tom1, tom2, floor tom, and overheads for cymbals. Vocal mics can be arranged left-to-right as the engineer sees them. Notice how all instruments and all vocals are located in their specific areas of the board. Now anyone, even a visiting engineer, will be able to navigate such a familiar layout in any situation.

Fader Stuff

For live applications, it is important to keep the channels requiring the most control on one fader layer. You do not want to change layers to control levels, because you can easily forget where you are. Usually a board with 32 channel faders can accommodate most of the sources I listed. If not, or if I only have 16 or 24 channel faders, I can use extra layers to group instruments that don't usually require individual adjustment. This gets us into some constructive creativity with *fader linking* or *DCA grouping* (if DCAs are available).

Let's say I have a Yamaha LS9 digital mixer with only 16 channel faders but two fader layers, providing a total of 32 channels, and I need eight channels for drum mics alone. With the fader-linking feature, I can put the kick mic on channel 1 of the first layer and put the other seven on channels 17–23 on the second layer. Once the drum set is balanced out in the soundcheck, I can select *fader-link* for all eight channels in a group so that adjusting the one kick fader on the first layer will control the balance of all the others, even though I can't see them in the second layer. This saves seven channels on the first layer for other things.

If I have master DCA faders on a digital board, I could choose to put *all* the drum mics on channels 17–24 on the second layer and assign them all to DCA 1 for overall control with the DCA 1 fader. In both cases, I never have to switch out of the first channel layer to adjust the whole drum kit. Plus, I've again saved those channels on the first layer for primary sources requiring more independent control. In this manner, I can also control multiple choir or orchestra mics on other layers using one channel or DCA fader.

Linking of motorized faders on a digital might bring up a question. What if I have something like orchestra mics linked, but I need to alter a level for one or two mics on the fly? It would be a pain to have to switch to the related display, disable linking, and make the change, so Yamaha came up with a solution. Just press and hold the SEL button at the top of the channel to make your adjustment. This temporarily disables the link for that channel so it can be changed, then reestablishes the link at the new setting once the SEL button is released. You don't have to worry about this with DCA since its assignment acts as a separate remote control, and your individual faders are always free to adjust.

Though digitals are capable of endless parameter adjustments to suit your whims, I have found some easy and useful settings on Yamaha boards that may be applicable to your equipment and needs. These should provide a good starting point if you're not sure where to begin. There are also plenty of factory presets you can try if mine don't work for you.

Compressors

Due to extreme cost and space demands, we were never in a position to demand compressors on every channel with affordable analog consoles. Now it's hard to imagine not having them, since they make our job easier and duplicate the sophisticated control we've been accustomed to in major studio applications. Even if I have singers or an engineer who can't balance, a proper setting on compressors can hold vocalists to a good blend. I'll cover more about compressor terminology and specifics in Chapter 8. For now, here are some basic settings you can try:

Lead singers: Threshold = –15dB to –5dB, Ratio = 5:1, Attack = 10ms, Release = 100ms, Knee = 5, Output = 0dB. (If you need a touch more level, bring up the compressor output.)

Background singers: same settings, except Threshold is set 5dB lower than lead. (This keeps their collective level just under lead vocals.)

Instruments could start the same as lead singers, but change drums, percussion, or bass to Knee = 2 or 3, Attack = 1ms, and Release = 10ms.

Pastor and other speaking mics: Threshold = –20dB to –15dB depending on their voice dynamics. (Some may go from a whisper to a scream.) Everything else is the same as lead vocals. This should keep their level more consistent and avoid blasting the audience.

*(Note: Compression isn't normally essential for live choir, piano, orchestra, and CD playback channels, but can be set the same as lead singers. Also, compressors are normally defaulted as **pre-fader,** so you will get consistent compression effect regardless of your fader level adjustments. The mixer may offer an internal patch option for post-fader compression if you really want it.)*

Main/Stereo output (recording): Threshold = 0dB, Ratio = 2:1, Attack = 30ms, Release = 90ms, Knee = 5, Output = +3dB.

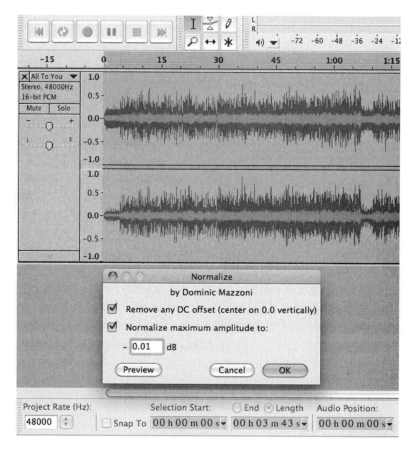

In recording, you have to be careful to get a good final mix level without squashing the sound. You want to get close to max without peaking out. Once your mix is finished, audio editing software and CDR mastering units usually have a **normalize** function that will set maximum levels for your final disc or audio files. So the above parameters are only a decent setting I discovered that can top off peaks with very subtle compression and give you a visual indication when you're around max level. To check this level, go to the Stereo output's compressor display and you should see only minimal (1 to 3 bars) meter indication of gain reduction (GR) with the loudest segments. If this is too much compression or you see your stereo meter peaking, bring down your mix levels to reduce the stereo output level. Don't try to max it out. When needed, let normalization automatically do that work for you.

Main output protection (live sound): Threshold = 0dB, Ratio = INF (infinity), Attack = 1ms, Release = 100ms, Knee = 4 or 5, Output = 0dB.

Stage monitors: Same as Main, but Threshold can be set as low as –10dB to control peaks.

Digital Effects

Just like standalone digital effects that have been around for decades, these internal units operate in the same way, and there are a lot of good factory presets to choose from. One useful practice in live sound for getting a good aux recording mix is to route one effects unit to that dedicated send mix for the sole purpose of simulating a natural room reverberation. You do this by going to that effect's return channel, leaving its fader level down (so it won't output elsewhere), and setting a *pre-fader* send level being sent to the recorder (let's say Send #8) at "0" or unity gain. Now any channel brought up in the dedicated send for that effect's input (let's say Send #6) will provide reverb on the recording for that channel. You can set that send level higher for a violin channel for a concert hall effect, and set it lower for a lead vocal so it doesn't clutter the lyrics. Experiment. The same applies if you are using a **stereo pair** link for

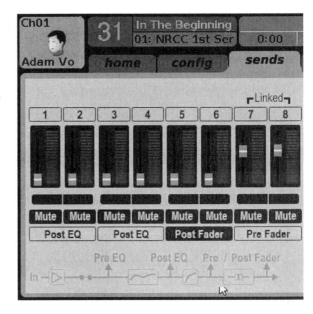

two sends. The stereo effects return would simply send stereo reverb out the two linked sends (like Send #7 and #8 in the illustration). If you are using another effect, like echo, for the live sound in the room, that effect's return can also be brought up in the recording send(s) so it is both recorded and live.

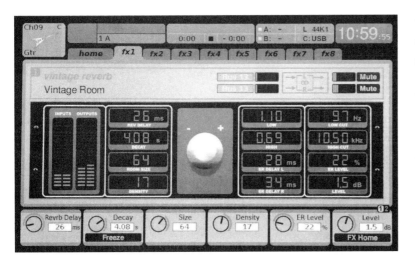

Depending on how large I want the room to sound, I'll set the **Reverb** or **Decay Time** at 2–2.5 seconds, and any **Pre-Delay** (**Reverb Delay**) and **ER** (**Early Reflection**) delay to around 50ms to provide depth and separation like a 1,000-seat room. Diffusion or density (the "thickness" of the reverb) is set high for a smooth and dense effect.

Scene vs. Manual Control

Scene memory is an invaluable asset for saving and recalling numerous setups, but it should not be overused in live applications to the point of circumventing our brain's higher capacity for spontaneous discretion. The digital mixer still responds and should be used much like an analog.

In ministry applications, for instance, scenes should be used to automatically get everything to a proper starting point, and then your ears will guide you through needed manual adjustments as the program progresses. When your program follows the same format on a daily or weekly basis, you don't need various engineers constantly storing new scenes for every program and even parts of a program. This can quickly lead to inconsistencies in performance, the opposite of what you'd expect from a digital mixer.

My choice is to have named, saved, and protected scenes for each different event, such as traditional and contemporary services, a Bible study, a preschool program, weddings, etc. These become the start point for a particular event's rehearsal. At rehearsal, I select the appropriate scene and copy it to another designated location, which will then be adjusted and used for the actual program. I will usually leave this temporary scene unprotected so I will be free to alter and store any adjustments I feel necessary, during rehearsal or performance. Often, no adjustments are needed and the rest is manual control.

Once that event is over, it is typically unnecessary to save this temporary scene, and I can use that location next week to copy another "start scene" for the next rehearsal. Every volunteer knows these start scenes and where their temporary event scene is stored, so everyone is on the same page and can substitute when necessary.

If I want only the pastor's mic active for the sermon, I could store a simple "Sermon" scene to be recalled each time, or simply mute the other channels. Digitals have mute groups (or DCA mutes), so only one or two button pushes can mute everything. In other words, the key to live digital mixing is maintaining a comfortable balance of automation and manual control. As with most things, keep it as simple as possible, and let your ears do most of the mixing.

In theatre, I need scene recalls only for crucial changes and maybe special effects. If I'm running 12–16 wireless mics, it can be tough remembering them all as we move through quick scene changes. So I create mixer scenes for each scene of a play that will recall proper starting levels for all the applicable mics and cut off all the other mics from the previous scene. I can then control the mics manually as the dialogue progresses. With good compression settings that help maintain comfortable levels (even in the event of an onstage scream), mics often need only minor adjustments while the actors control most of their dynamics. And if someone walks off stage during the scene, I just bring the fader down. No need for another scene. I can also name the mixer scenes as the page numbers of the script so when I get to the clearly indicated point on Page 20, I know to hit the Page 20 scene recall. Common sense rules the day.

Cause & Effect

TRYING TO KEEP UP WITH NEW EFFECTS devices is like trying to track the federal deficit—five minutes later, you're out of touch and it's over the edge! Frankly, I don't relish my whole life becoming a successive parade of new-product learning curves. Give me at least a few meager minutes for coffee and Fox News.

Seriously though, it is truly amazing the quality and flexibility of today's digital effects. But to be practical and avoid a section rivaling Tolstoy's *War and Peace*, let me just give you a few meager minutes of basic descriptions and tips on the more common ones. I also have demonstrations of some of these effects on the book's downloadable sample tracks.

DELAY

Delay is considered a single repeat of an original signal with 0% **feedback** (or **FB.GAIN** in this graphic), and with delay time designated in milliseconds (ms). A delay of 10–40ms can fatten up a vocal, 40–100ms gives the slap-back effect of small to medium rooms (popular in the recordings of the '50s), and 100–

250ms simulates larger-room delays. Longer times are not very natural short of the Grand Canyon, so they are used primarily for special effects.

In recording, I sometimes like to use a quality delay unit to stereo-image a mono source. Just pan the original source's channel to one side, bring up its aux send to the delay unit, set the delay at 10ms, and pan its effect return channel to the opposite side, making sure it is *100 percent effect* with no original signal mixed in. You can adjust the send level so the meter levels are pretty much the same for both sides, left and right.

You might notice something unusual, though. If both original and delay are set to the same meter levels, the original side still sounds a bit louder. This is called the ***Haas effect***. If a separate delayed signal is within 40ms of the original, the sound will be perceived as coming more from the direction of the first signal to reach you—the original signal—by a mere 10ms. The Haas effect fools your ears. (We'll find out later that the Haas effect has a very useful purpose in large-room sound-system setups.)

For this purpose of stereo-imaging a mono source, the slight perception of imbalance may not be important, but you can bring up the delay level about 3dB more if you feel it necessary. Either way, you will notice a nice stereo imaging to that mono source.

(Note: This stereo effect is demonstrated in the audio tracks available for download with this book.)

ECHO

An echo is a delay with decaying repeats. Adjustments of **feedback** or **regeneration,** as the repeats are called, are in percentages. I only use 15–25 percent for smooth 200ms echoes with three to four repeats. I often prefer using quarter-note-triplet echoes in music for a subtler echo on lead guitar and vocals because it will be more noticeable between the beats without overdoing the echo level. (If you don't understand triplets, swallow your pride and ask a musician or music director to provide guidance.) Many echo units, including guitar pedals, also offer a manual TAP function button. This allows you to tap the button in time with music so the echo repeats are set to the beat of that particular song, especially nice for trailing echoes off a vocal or giving electric guitar parts a very smooth *keyboard pad* type of sound.

REVERB

Reverb is extremely short echoes, or multiple reflections, so numerous that they create a dense and continuous effect that gradually decays. Natural reverb times for a good concert hall are 2 to 2.5 seconds long. A **pre-delay** setting, which simulates the delayed wall reflection preceding reverberation in a large room, can be set for 50–100ms to give the reverb more depth and slightly distance it from the original signal for clarity.

There are different types of reverbs to simulate various room characteristics, namely **Hall, Chamber,** and **Room**. Another more synthetic type is **Plate**, a brighter-sounding effect simulating the large metal plate reverbs of yesteryear, and **Gated** (or **Reverse Gate**) reverb, with an abrupt cutoff of the decay as if shut down by a noise gate. This was made popular on drums by Phil Collins of Genesis, and short versions make for an interesting "dense-delay" effect.

In popular music production, I reduce the bass frequencies of reverb in varying degrees to avoid smearing the low end of the mix. This *low-cut* or *HPF* can be set anywhere from 100Hz to 200Hz within the reverb unit itself, or taken out on the reverb unit's return channel EQ (if available).

MODULATED EFFECTS

Chorus is a lush effect that delays and modulates a pitch around the original note. I don't recommend it on vocals except for a special effect, but it's really nice on instruments like guitars, where it adds color and fullness. It can make a 6-string guitar sound more like a 12-string. **Flange** (I call it chorus with an attitude) is a short delayed chorus regenerated through itself to produce a more radical and hollow-sounding effect.

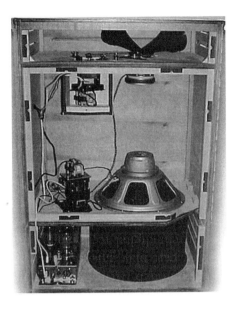

Leslie simulation is another nice chorus variation based on the Doppler effect of the Leslie rotating speakers used with the classic Hammond organs. If you've ever noticed how the pitch of a train or a fast car changes as it moves toward and away from you, that is the same effect you get as the Leslie horn and speaker baffle spin. It is actually a unique combination of **chorus** (pitch going up and down), **tremolo** (level going up and down), and tone; all these elements change as the sound shifts from shooting toward you to away from you. Leslie simulation is merely an electronic version of the effect. Another feature of a Leslie effect is a control (or footswitch) to gradually speed up and slow down the modulation, mimicking the Leslie's speaker motors as they were switched between slow and fast. I have used two early 1970s versions for guitar: a compact cabinet version called the Leslie 16, as used by Stevie Ray Vaughan and others, and the first pedal model called a PEI Junior. Loved it!

PITCH SHIFT

This one is pretty self-explanatory. It changes the pitch of a note to a selected interval, which stays constant, unlike chorus, which modulates around the note. Coarse adjustment is in *half-step* (semitone) note increments, and fine adjustments are in percentages of a half-step. With a fine adjustment of 10–15 percent, you get an effect similar to chorus but cleaner, especially for vocal, since it doesn't wave around like chorus. Coarse adjustment of two to five half-steps on a vocal tends to get you into a higher "munchkin" or lower "demonic" sounding effect.

I call this "stupid" pitch shift, because we also have **intelligent pitch shift,** which goes a step further. You can select a root key and a musical scale or mode, and the pitch will follow musical notes in specific harmony intervals, allowing you to sing or play in harmony with yourself! Popular units offering this include the TC Electronics Helicon and Digitech Vocalizers.

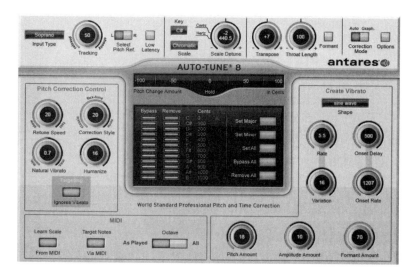

In addition, there are high-quality, dedicated **pitch correctors** (also known as auto-tune) like Antares and Melodyne software programs that will actually correct a singer's pitch in real time. (These are used *direct* like signal processors, not *sidechain* like the other effects.) It's getting to the point where, if you can't carry a tune in a bucket, you can dump it from a pitch corrector! These are more for studio use, and should be used with discernment for subtle correction during the recording process while being aware of the potential for unnatural artifacts. They should never be used as a fix for lazy engineering or bad singers. I recall a studio that had recorded an awesome demo for a pretty lame singer using pitch correction, and he actually got signed to a record deal! Imagine their shock when they got him into the studio and he could barely sing. You can bet the A&R rep who signed him was soon flipping burgers at McDonald's.

There are many other special effects, such as distortion, ring modulation, phasing, wah-wah, auto-panning, sampling, multi-tap echo, et-et-et-et cetera. There's a bazillion things you can do with these and combinations of effects that will require your own dedicated experimentation. I guess this is something like bungee jumping. It may be intimidating at first, but the results can be exhilarating. Or it may scare the begeebees out of you. (Imagine that, I've sunk to *bazillion* and *begeebees* in the same paragraph!)

Signal Corps

TO BBE OR NOT TO BBE . . .

Signal processing, if you'll remember, is a direct hookup that affects the whole signal. It can provide tremendous benefits, but you rarely get something for nothing (unless you're a politician). Any time you process something, you can travel a little further from its natural state. Maybe its natural state sounds like garbage, so you have nothing to lose. But if it sounds decent, the trick is to get it through the system with as little mangling as possible. I've actually had recording clients come into the studio with one concern on their minds—how many graphic equalizers I had. "Sure, I do all my critical recording on a 1985 Tascam Cassette Portastudio, but my 22 graphic EQs make it sound like gold!" (Take me out in the back and shoot me.)

Signal processing should never be a crutch for poor engineering or system design. Often it's a necessary element to help control levels for recording or to tune a room for optimal sound quality, and the advent of digital processing has eliminated much of our "mangling" concerns from the negatives of analog circuitry and interfacing. But in many instances, there are better alternatives. Try a different mic, better speakers, improved mixer EQ technique—milk it for all it's worth before you patch in another device. When it is time, here are some of your choices . . .

AURAL ENHANCERS

Since I so cleverly used **BBE** in the header to make a point, I figured I should probably elaborate with some history. BBE was a popular and economical sonic processor that could improve the clarity and dimension of an analog recording, a trait called "transparency" in which the instruments and vocals stand out more clearly. With current digital technology, you can easily achieve this without a BBE, but it sure helped me through a lot of earlier recording projects, and with some great results.

One aspect of the BBE's historical design is worth noting. It improved clarity by actually delaying the mid and low frequencies by a few milliseconds so the high frequencies would reach you first. This made them stand out more clearly due to different, yet imperceptible, timing. It's an interesting approach which also helped me understand how sound innovations can work with speaker systems. You might detect this concept in some of my later discussions.

Another enhancement processor is the **aural exciter**. This one adds narrowband high harmonics for a sweet high end, particularly for

vocals. It uses some harmonic distortion to achieve the effect, so, unlike the BBE, which was a totally clean effect, aural exciters are used more on individual sources, like vocals, to give them an appealing high-end edge and "breathiness." Radio stations also use it to enhance their broadcast quality. Like the BBE, you don't hear about these tools as much anymore due to the sonic superiority of digital mixing, but they still have their place for certain applications and personal preferences.

GRAPHIC EQ

A professional **graphic equalizer** breaks down the frequencies we studied into 15 to 31 separate controls, allowing us to adjust them individually. Graphics are used primarily in live sound to correct for room acoustics and speaker-response deficiencies, and there are some easy clues for me as to when a system is well tuned: a professional artist CD should sound near-studio quality (allowing for room reverberation, of course) played through the system with its channel EQ set to flat, and a quality handheld vocal mic set flat should sound clear and natural at about 6 inches. (If closer, the proximity effect of unidirectionals makes them sound a bit "bassy" prior to rolling out low EQ.)

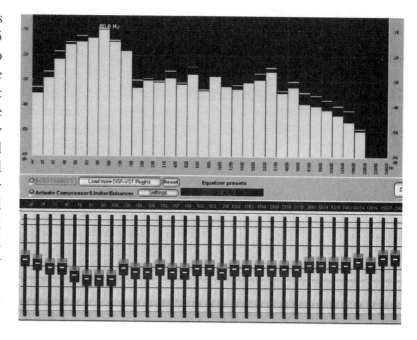

Graphics include a level control for maintaining **unity gain**. Once all the equalization is set, hit the Bypass switch to see if the perceived level changes due to your EQ settings. If it does, you can adjust the level control so it's equal when you switch back and forth. This maintains proper levels through the system without loss or undue increase.

Since room and speaker anomalies are so varied, no one can tell you how to set a graphic EQ. I have found that many rooms have boomy or muddy problems around 100–160Hz and 315–400Hz, respectively, and horns may need control anywhere from 3kHz to 8kHz to smooth out peaks or harshness. Feedback frequencies also need to be addressed. If you want to get more accurate settings, read on.

Real-time Analyzer (RTA): This is a device designed to help you determine accurate response for your speakers. It's not a signal processor, but it needs mentioning here since it will help you set up a graphic equalizer. This unit has a broad LED or meter readout corresponding to all the frequencies of the graphic EQ, a calibrated microphone for picking up all those frequencies, and a *pink noise* generator. Pink noise is all frequencies produced simultaneously and equally, as our ears perceive it, and sounds like what it implies—noise. Like a roomful of people all talking at the same time. Or maybe just your mother-in-law.

There's a tactic to using an analyzer. A good studio monitor has *flat* (accurate) response as measured usually within 1 meter in its specifications. Add another speaker and you get more bass from *coupling*. Move farther away, and you lose high end from absorption in the air. Therefore, if I analyze combinations of speakers from too great a distance, I'll set the EQ for too much highs and not enough bass. (Think about it, or take my word for it.)

To balance things out, I find a spot to place the analyzer mic within the dispersion pattern of one speaker (or a tight group), and no more than 50 feet back because live sound speakers are designed to project much farther than studio monitors. Since any subwoofers being used are more omnidirectional, I just make sure I'm also in a decent spot to pick up their low end. With the graphic EQ for the system set to flat, pink noise is run into a channel and brought up through the speakers to an average expected performance volume. Now the pink noise, mixer, and amps constitute a "flat" signal. Any discrepancies read by the analyzer can, for all practical purposes, be attributed to the speakers, or room, or both.

Mic sensitivity is set on the analyzer to a point where the meter levels are equally distributed on either side of the center line. Individual graphic EQ frequencies are then adjusted up or down opposite the analyzer, bringing the meters as close to a flat center line as possible. This corrects speaker response and compensates for major room resonances and reflections.

Afterward, you'll analyze stage monitors at close range and then check for any consistent feedback problems by bringing up mics and subtly tuning any graphics as needed to minimize major feedback problems. As you can guess, an RTA can be a good investment and a great aid in developing a "golden ear." Standalone RTA units were made by Goldline, Rane, and DOD, and you can still find them on eBay, but now analyzers are often included as component features in digital mixers and signal processors. There are also a few smartphone apps like Spectrum Analyzer and FrequenSee that you can try for minor tuning needs, but don't expect them to be as accurate as dedicated units or software for major tuning of systems.

COMPRESSOR/LIMITER

You're running sound when suddenly the singer hits a high note that does a light show on your meters and turns your tweeters into confetti. You have three choices: shoot the singer, take up needlepoint, or add another set of helping hands—the **compressor/limiter**.

Compression gently controls level, where **limiting** aggressively stops it. The **ratio** control determines which occurs. A 1:1 ratio setting means that for every 1dB of signal coming in, 1dB is getting out—no change, no compression. A 4:1 ratio means that for every 4dB of signal coming in, only 1dB is getting out—one-fourth the peak we would have gotten otherwise. Anything greater than 10:1 is considered limiting. A **threshold** control sets the desired level at which the compressor will be activated, and our new hands are ready to start grabbing peaks. Other controls include input and output levels, **attack** and **release** to adjust reaction time and duration, and **knee** to soften the effect by having the compression start a little early and increase gradually so it won't suddenly squash the sound. Check manuals for more details.

In the studio, I rarely use compression on sources other than vocals and guitars because I like to maintain natural dynamics, and many instrument peaks are due to resonant frequencies, which I can control with EQ. Always use such processing sparingly; too much will destroy dynamics and clarity. I don't recommend using a compressor on an overall recording mix unless it's a quality tube model or part of digital mastering software, and only then at a mild 2:1 ratio. (Tubes and high-resolution digital are kinder and gentler.)

In live sound, I often use compression on most sources to gently control spontaneous peaks, since digital mixers have provided this awesome convenience. Limiting is used more for protection. It can be applied to main and monitor mixer outputs to avoid overdriving amplifiers and speakers. The threshold is set so that limiting starts just prior to amplifier clipping (overload). Where compression uses a more gradual "soft knee" response representing a more rounded threshold curve, limiting has a harder response (sometimes called "brick wall") to minimize the effect under the threshold. Many amplifiers also have some form of clip-limiting built in. I recommend using it if it's available.

NOISE GATE

A noise gate is an automatic on/off switch. Again, you have a **threshold**, but this one is set at a minimum level where the gate should cut in. When used on a mic channel, a low or absent signal triggers the gate to cut off the mic so nothing else bleeds through.

A simple gate is generally found on most analog compressor/limiters. More complex dedicated units and digital processors will have adjustable **attack**, **hold**, **decay**, or **rate** controlling opening and closing time and duration, as well as **floor** or **range** to adjust a gate so that it never fully closes. A slow attack delays opening so that you might minimize a problem at the start of a sound, like an overly peaky "slap" bass guitar part, though compression can control this, too. A slow decay or rate will avoid noticeable cutoff of a gradually decaying sound, like cymbals.

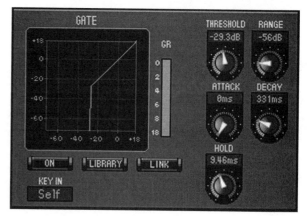

DIGITAL SIGNAL PROCESSORS

Now take every piece of equipment we've talked about in the last two chapters, add some basic mixer and metering functions, digitize it, put it all in a box with audio and computer connections, and you'll have the new generation of **DSP** (**D**igital **S**ignal **P**rocessing). Just like digital mixers, we now have almost unlimited flexibility with the components and configurations of total-system processing.

The first time I used a DSP unit, I had to laugh. I was sitting on my couch at home with the DSP software manager in a laptop, designing a sound system for a customer. I was dragging all types of audio gear onto the screen: meters, routing mixers, graphic equalizers, compressors, room delay, multi-effects, you name it. I felt like I was playing a video game!

By the time I was finished, I had a $25,000 processing system assembled in a $5,000 box. When I got to the facility, I downloaded my "video game" from the computer into the box, hooked up all the audio connections, fired up the system, and everything worked like a charm. I was sold! In fact, I ended up needing one more piece of gear in the system, which would have cost another $1,000 and taken at least a couple of days to get shipped in. I just dragged it onto the screen, connected a couple of "virtual cables," and I was done.

Peavey actually started this trend back in the 1990s with their Media Matrix system, and now most major sound manufacturers have some sort of live sound DSP available, whether as standalone units or in their digital mixers. Some lower-cost models (under $1,000) have fixed configurations with fewer connections, maybe two inputs and six outputs like the DBX DriveRack series. Bigger models, like the BSS BLU or Yamaha DME, have extensive programming to design and control more elements as well as input/output options. These units also allow you to store and recall different scenes, like their mixer counterparts. One DSP unit alone can control feeds to mains, monitors, audio and video recording,

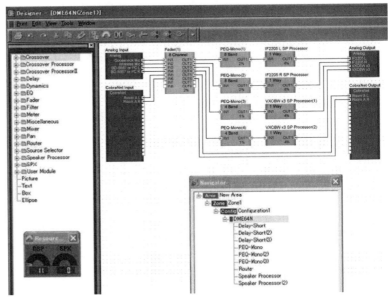

balconies, underbalconies, hallways, lobbies, and hearing assistance systems. Then each memorized scene can be programmed to control which systems are on and how they're set for any given performance or function. Some can even be networked to other DSP units spread around a huge facility so they all act as one. Yes, the complexities of these units are best left to professionals, but they are great tools in everything from churches to major arenas and concert halls.

Be aware that most of these digital processing features are included in the larger digital mixers, so you won't necessarily need both. I'm now able to design most of my systems with all signals going straight from digital mixer to amplifiers. One DSP item typically missing in digital mixers is an **electronic crossover**, but these are often available in professional amplifier designs internally or as an add-on option. Also, powered speaker systems will have their own active crossovers and amplifiers built in. Crossovers require an understanding of amplification and speaker components, so I choose to cover them in Chapter 10, "Pumping Paper."

TUBE PROCESSORS

I might also mention the continuing interest in **tube processing,** both with audio enthusiasts and discriminating guitarists. Now, with the stark reality of digital recording, tubes are often in demand for the unique warmth and "harmonic smoothing" they can offer. You might compare it to the visual difference between video and film, where video is sharp but film has an appealing "softness"—call it classic, artsy, or intimate. Tube equipment like mic preamps, compressors, and EQs cost more than their solid-state varieties, but are worth the expense when you're trying to achieve some unique results in your studio applications.

In a similar way, current high-resolution digital mixers and processors offer distinct advantages over most of their analog predecessors due to the smoothness of the waveform and the absence of phase shift and distortion associated with analog equipment and integration. Think of this digital sound like HD video with the capacity for stunning clarity. It all depends on what you're looking for in your sound. Tube or digital, audio processing today has reached a remarkable high point in history.

Power Tools

NO PAIN, NO GAIN

This is the macho section, dealing with devices of sheer brute force . . . heavy current draw . . . massive gain . . . shattered speakers . . . Tim Allen, eat your heart out! Amplifiers take our measly signals from the mixer and boost them enough to move speakers and, hopefully, our sense of good taste. Pro amps can provide power of 200 to 2,000 watts or more. These are the most powerful electronic devices you will use, and they possess the potential for doing the most damage. You want the right amp for your application and enough power for your needs without overloading anything along the way.

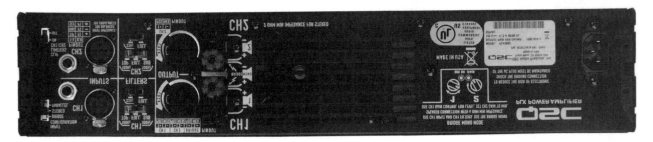

So Watt!

How much wattage is enough? Loose answers are based on several factors: "How many vocals/instruments do I have? Am I amplifying bass or drums? What are the capabilities of my speakers? How large an area do I need to cover?" (See, now I'm talking to myself.)

Let me just throw you some rough ideas in this area. The bare minimum I need is about 100 watts per channel stereo for near-field monitors in a small studio. In live sound, one watt per person of room capacity is a reasonable starting point for main speakers, especially in small churches and performance venues. This should cover minimal needs at moderate volume—six to eight channels of vocals and light rhythm instruments (guitar, keyboard, CD playback, kazoo, spoons, etc.). Increase total wattage proportionately to room and audience size. Stage monitors should be fine with as little as 200 watts per channel.

For more powerful club and concert levels, including contemporary worship in churches, I suggest 2 watts per person minimum (3 watts if subwoofers are employed) should be available, with speakers and subs suited to the task. You can rarely have too much power, so your budget will keep you within a practical range. The good news is that it can cost as little as $100 more to increase your power by 50 percent with current amp technology, so don't skimp unnecessarily on such a crucial need.

Keep in mind, though, that this decision process needs to be implemented in reverse. We want to design a speaker system that meets the needs of the venue(s) we will perform in, whether installation or touring. Then the speaker system and its specifications will designate the amplification we will need to power it. I would want to have at least 10 percent more power than specified to assure headroom and clean amplification that won't peak out at nominal levels.

Sound Pressure

Now we need to understand how we hear these wattage differences. *SPL*, or sound pressure level, represents these differences in **decibels** (**dBs**) relative to the way we hear sound. Where only about 10 percent of people can hear a 1dB change in level, around 50 percent of people can hear a 2dB change, and just about anybody can hear a 3dB change. (Most audio knob adjustments are notched in 3dB increments because it assures a noticeable change.)

Now the real kicker—it takes double the amp power to change the level only 3dB, but you need a 10dB increase to double the perceived level! Consequently, if we have a 100-watt system, we need to get close to 800 watts to sound twice as loud! (Crazy, ain't it?) But that's if it depended on the amp alone, which it doesn't. As with wattage, doubling the number of speakers can also yield a 3dB increase. In that case, getting up to 400 watts with twice as many speakers should add a total of about 9dB. Keep this in mind as you assess your level needs. We'll cover more about SPL and speaker efficiency in Chapter 10.

CHECKS & BALANCES

Amps take signals coming in and boost them tremendously, including any noise or *ground loops*. So it's the same situation as the mixer input stage—*balanced* inputs can become crucial. Again, they eliminate noise picked up along the length of the cable and allow you to lift grounds that cause hum. Unless all your equipment is situated close together, you shouldn't use an amp with unbalanced inputs. Otherwise, Murphy's Law dictates that you will have problems. Wiring connections are the same as we discussed earlier.

Setting Level

As with mixers, the level controls on the amp should be set properly for the system. When our mixer reaches around 0dB *unity gain* on its meters (or around –6dB on a digital mixer with full 0dB meters), an amplifier cut all the way up to "0" should be running at full power. Then, when the mixer hits a little above that, we should start to see overload indication on the amp. With this setup, we will always know how hard our system is working by our meter readings. But if we have plenty of power for our system and room, we shouldn't have to run our amps at max level. It is best to retain optimal mixer levels and simply cut the amps back to a maximum comfortable listening level.

An easy way to check maximum amp levels without breaking glassware is to unhook the speakers from the amp. (Don't do this with a tube amp!) With strong music or pink noise from an analyzer running through the mixer, bring up the master level until the meter hits +3dB (–3dB on digital mixers). Of course, all processors—like equalizers and crossovers—should be set for unity gain so you don't lose level along the way. Then bring up the amp level until you see its **overload**, or **clipping**, indicator just start to illuminate. That's your setting. Now you can cut off the test source, hook up your speakers, and repeat after me: "I will not push my meters over the limit. I know that is all

the power I have. I do not want to blow my speakers and spend lots of money on repairs. Thank you Mr. White for saving my equipment. I'm sending $100 cash to show my appreciation."

Again, if the system is too loud for your needs with optimal meter levels, drop back the amp levels instead of the mixer to a volume that is comfortable. This will give you a better signal-to-noise ratio through the lines. You can make note of the higher amp settings for future reference in case you need to crank it up for a stronger program. If you can't quite get the amp to overload with the above procedure, you have my permission to raise graphic EQ or active crossover levels slightly to the point where it does. If it still won't, it's an indication you have a level problem or mismatched equipment. Ask a pro for help in finding the best solution.

Ohm, Sweet Ohm

Amplifier power is rated in relation to the amount of power draw by the speakers. It's listed in the specifications of the amp and determined by the impedance of the speaker load. You will see *dual* or *stereo* amp wattages based on **8Ω** (ohms), **4Ω**, and sometimes **2Ω** loads, and they should correspond to what your speakers can handle if you expect to drive them to full power. (More speakers are damaged by too little power than they are by too much due to the extra stress caused by trying to reproduce a distorted amp signal.) There's also a rating called **bridged mono**, which we'll discuss shortly.

STEREO MODE (Both channels driven)	
8Ω/ FTC 20 Hz – 20 kHz / 0.1% THD	185 W
4Ω/ FTC 20 Hz – 20 kHz / 0.1% THD	280 W
2Ω/ FTC 20 Hz – 20 kHz / 1% THD	–
BRIDGE-MONO MODE	
8Ω/ FTC 20 Hz – 20 kHz / 0.1% THD	530 W
4Ω/ EIA 1 kHz / 1% THD	830 W
Signal to Noise (20 Hz – 20 kHz) 8Ω	> -100 dB
Distortion (SMPTE-IM)	< 0.01%
Output Circuitry	Class AB
SHIPPING	
Weight	35 lb (15.9 kg)
Net	41 lb (18.6 kg)

Most speakers are 8Ω and will indicate it near their connector plate. If you connect two 8Ω speakers to the same amp, the load halves and becomes 4Ω. You'll notice in amp specs that the wattage on a 4Ω load is often around two-thirds higher than 8Ω. So for the extra speaker we add, the amp provides more power. By the same token, two 4Ω loads make a 2Ω. However, the limit is usually 4Ω for most amps; below that, they may eventually overheat and shut down. If the total speaker impedance load is too low, you will need more amps to accommodate them.

I will even go so far as to give you the only formula I intend to in this book:

Impedance = R1 x R2

R1 + R2

R1 equals the impedance of one speaker, and R2 equals that of a second.

For example, if we have an 8Ω and a 4Ω speaker: 8 x 4 = 32 and 32 ÷ 12 = 2.67Ω

8 + 4 = 12

Obviously, this is too low for a minimum rating of 4Ω. So use this formula to make sure you're not overtaxing your amplifiers.

Amp Modes

Most professional amps are designed as stereo, or dual, amplifiers—they will operate in stereo or as two individual amps in one package. Consequently, each amp can handle its own load for discrete purposes, like one side for mains and the other side for subwoofers or stage monitors. Most have a special switch for different modes of operation. These include:

Stereo or Dual—each ch.annel of the amp receives its own source and can function independently of the other side.

Parallel—the inputs of both amps are connected so they receive a common source typically from the first channel (CH 1, CH A, or Left), though each amp's level setting and impedance load is still independent.

Bridged Mono—both amps are electronically combined to form one BIG amp. *This is not meant as a designation for "non-stereo" applications!*

This mode is for rare occasions when you have a speaker or subwoofer requiring more power than one channel of an amp can provide. If I wish to drive one 500-watt, 8Ω speaker with an amp of 250 watts per channel at 4Ω, I can switch it to Bridged Mono and turn it into a single 500-watt amp at 8Ω. (And now for my next trick . . .) Only the first channel of the amp provides input and level in this mode. Be advised, however, that most amps are rated only to 8Ω in bridged mode, and there is a special method of hooking up the speakers. I'll explain that in the Connectors section below, but to make sure you get it right, please refer to your owner's manual for bridging specifics.

70V Lines

In installations like churches or office buildings, you can end up with a mess of little speakers all over the place in ceilings, on walls, under balconies, wherever! This obviously causes a problem with total impedance, so the audio geeks of yesteryear came up with another idea. A 70V connection is designated

on amplifiers that accommodate it, and the connection must be used with speakers equipped with 70V transformers. They are designed exclusively for this application.

These speakers have separate wire taps off their transformer for different wattages that we choose for the speaker to draw depending on how much level we need. Since they are usually 8-inch speakers for covering small areas, the taps can range from 1/4 to 10 watts. In this situation, we are concerned with total wattage

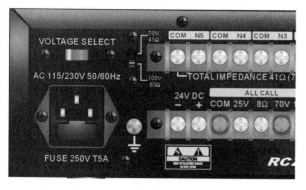 

consumption instead of impedance. With a 50-watt amp, we can run up to 10 speakers wired at 5 watts each: 10 x 5 = 50. Or 25 speakers at 2 watts each. Simple math. For the latter, we can run a speaker line paralleled from the amp to the COM (or C, for *common*) and 2-watt taps on all 25 speakers. If you want particular speakers to be louder (maybe because they're in a noisier area), simply tap those at a higher wattage. Just make sure you tap *down* at least some of the other speakers to maintain a total load of no more than 50 watts. You can also purchase wallmount 70V attenuators to install in areas where you need variable control of the level. They will include wiring diagrams on how to hook them into the speaker line.

CONNECTORS & CABLES

Amp inputs are generally the same **RCA phono**, **1/4-inch phone**, or **XLR** connections found on mixers. On amp outputs and speaker inputs, connections include **1/4-inch phone** plugs, **Neutrik Speakon** connectors, or **5-way binding posts**. All have specific wiring for positive and negative connections. **Speakons** are durable, four- to eight-conductor plugs designed to accommodate professional amps and enclosures, including bi-amped, multiwire connections. **Binding posts** have screw-down caps allowing the connection of bare wire through a hole in the side of their metal posts, or the insertion of **dual banana plugs** at the head of the caps. Be aware that banana plugs also have positive and negative indication for their posts, usually a tab sticking out on the negative side of the plug. As with all plugs, make sure you

get the +/- polarity right for these connections.

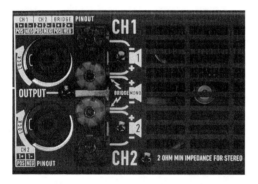

For each channel of a dual amp, there will be a red post for the *positive* (+) side and a black post for the *negative* (–) side of the connection. In **Bridged Mono** mode, the red post of the first channel will be the positive, and the red post of the second channel will be the negative. Always double-check your manual for proper connections.

Large-gauge cable is used to carry the higher voltage output of amplifiers. Wires are run side by side like electrical cables and are not shielded like mic and line cables. For different types of speaker cable, there will be some conspicuous difference between the two wires so you can keep positive and negative straight on each end: copper/silver wires, two-color insulation, ribbed/smooth coating on lamp-cord style, etc. Figuring for a single speaker from a 100- to 400-watt amp, I suggest a minimum of 16-gauge for cables up to 25 feet, 14 gauge up to 50 feet, and 12-gauge up to 100 feet. If in doubt or for larger amps, always go to the next larger gauge.

Going Through a Phase: I can't tell you how many times I have been to a performance or in a studio and heard speakers wired out of phase. Avoiding this just involves making sure all the positive and negative connections of your speakers are hooked to the same on the amps. *Double check yourself.* Otherwise, your sound will be screwy.

Your ears can also alert you with a quick test. With music playing, start in front of and facing one speaker, then gradually move toward the other speaker. When you get equidistant between the two, sound should appear centered. But if it suddenly sounds as if everything is split to both sides, they're out of phase. It's most likely the cable connections unless you had Goober rewire your speaker cabinets.

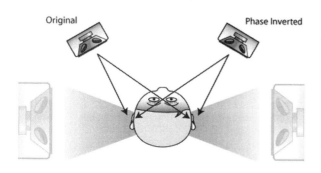

Original   Phase Inverted

If necessary, you can check to see whether passive (not active) speaker cabinets are internally wired properly. With a cable plugged into the cabinet, quickly touch the positive and negative contacts of a 9V battery to the corresponding points on the other end of the cable. (With a 1/4-inch phone plug, you can touch positive to the tip and negative to the sleeve.) If the woofer jumps forward, everything's okay. If it jumps backward, connections are reversed. If it jumps sideways, seek counseling. If you can't see the woofer or don't know what it is, forget this test and proceed to Chapter 10.

Proper polarity is important not only for the center imaging, but to avoid loss of overall response. Speakers out of phase are trying to cancel each other out. Once corrected, you'll notice better response from the whole system, and others will be amazed at your incredible ability to detect the problem. It's a good way to make new friends and an interesting topic at parties. Pass the chips.

AMP EXTRAS

Amplifiers often incorporate other features that aid our efforts and eliminate the need and cost of extra components. Low-cut switches allow us to roll sub-bass frequencies out of speakers that don't need it, like stage monitors and ceiling speakers. Variable low-cut and crossover filters in some models will switch amps to full-range or subwoofer modes for speaker systems so you can get by without an external crossover unit. This can be useful with digital mixers, which typically don't incorporate crossovers but can provide all the other signal processing needed from graphic EQs to limiting and even delayed outputs for underbalcony. (More on that later.) Then you can simply run straight from mixer to amps. In the case of powered speakers with their own internal amps and crossovers, you can run straight from mixer to speakers.

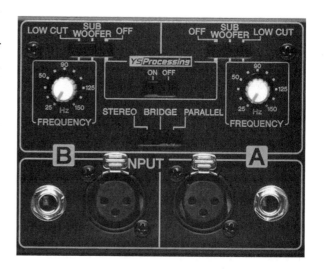

Amp limiters will protect equipment from overload, and some amps may include special speaker processing to optimize speaker response or efficiency. Finally, newer commercial designs are providing computer connection for comprehensive display and network control of an entire system of amplifiers from one central point.

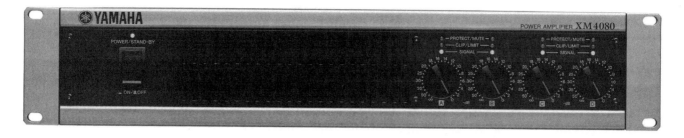

There are also a few multi-amp designs with four to six amplifiers in one package. Though they are typically lower-power versions, they save cost and space for moderate needs, such as monitors or 70V systems. Just be aware of some of these available options when you are shopping for an amplifier. They might save you a few hundred dollars.

Pumping Paper

10

IF THERE IS GOING TO BE A WEAK LINK in system design, it will likely be the speakers. This is because they have the most going against them. As with microphones, we are in a delicate position of transforming between electrical and acoustical energy. But microphones are single, small elements picking up within a relatively short distance, minimizing room for error. Speakers, however, use multiple large components that must blend together and cover large distances. Consequently, how well things are designed becomes vital.

S.P. L. & R.U.Def

SPL, or **sound pressure level**, which we touched on in the amp section as a reference to how we hear wattage changes, is a measurement of the actual intensity levels speakers can generate. It is based on a 0dB threshold of hearing, with normal conversation at about 70dB, a strong gospel church service around 100dB, and some rock concerts capable of 120dB or more. Anything over 105dB can start getting uncomfortable, depending on your tolerance, with 140dB considered the Official Threshold of Pain. (Actually, that starts at 120dB for most people.) Following are some of my examples of various levels (read from bottom up):

Threshold of Pain	140dB	Beginner violin lessons
	130dB	Aerosmith Concert
	120dB	Taylor Swift Concert
	110dB	Michael Buble Concert
	100dB	Least favorite TV commercial
	90dB	Threshold for teenager response
	80dB	Threshold of teenager's hearing
	70dB	Normal conversation
	60dB	Normal TV level
	50dB	Dog owner being dragged on asphalt
	40dB	Dog owner panting trying to keep up with dog
	30dB	Dog panting during morning walk
	20dB	Child's room when doing something they're not supposed to
	10dB	
Threshold of Hearing	0dB	Sound of critics praising this book

Our ears were actually designed for conversation. At speech levels, we have a peak in our hearing response around 3kHz, where the clarity is, while higher- and lower-end response is down considerably. In other words, we don't hear *flat* at lower levels. This is why many hi-fi systems have a **loudness** or **contour** switch. It's a boost for the low and high end to compensate for our low-level hearing response.

Yet an interesting thing happens when we start cranking up the volume. A little "compressor" in our brain starts grabbing the 3kHz spot while the other frequencies rise to catch up, until the response finally flattens out at around 90dB. That's why music sounds better when it's louder—our ears are hearing it right! (Sorry, Mom.)

For this reason, I usually run music closer to 90dB in the studio when I want to hear response more accurately. But I want to keep dynamic concert sound under 110dB to avoid hearing damage. The exception is low end, which I can drive to slightly higher "feel" levels, adding punch while avoiding excessive ear-damaging, high-frequency levels. Be aware, though, that long durations of any levels approaching 100dB and beyond can affect your hearing.

STACKING UP

Back in the old days (that's Woodstock for many of us), the norm was big and bunches. We had separate boxes for tweeters, horns, mids, mid bass, bass, and Boones Farm. (Don't ask.) We had four-way and five-way crossovers. Hundreds of pounds of amps. And "narly" sound, dude! That's because all these mixed-bag components were doing their own thing and could rarely get it together . . . just like us.

With the vast improvements in speaker design and components, we now have systems that actually work together, take up less real estate, and sound good. We can get everything we need from **two-way** or **three-way speakers** and **subwoofers**, but how do we know which ones to get? Good hints are in the specifications of speakers, but they need to be looked at collectively. For instance, with near-field studio monitors, I'm mostly concerned with the **frequency response**. Larger PA speakers should also be scrutinized for **sensitivity** and **polar response**.

Sensitivity

Now you can use all that stuff you learned about *SPL* where doubling-wattage-adds-3dB and 10dB-is-twice-as-loud. Studio monitors, which are designed more for close-up use and moderate levels, have sensitivity listings around 87dB. PA speakers are around 97dB, a 10dB increase. This means that if you hook up a PA speaker in place of a studio monitor without changing the amp or level settings, it will sound at least twice as loud. Obviously, this is much better for high-level applications. In fact, just a 3dB difference in speaker efficiency can mean an increase comparable to doubling amp wattage. Remember?

Frequency Response

So if we see one PA speaker listed at 97dB and another at 100dB, buy the second one, right? Wrong! First, you need to look at the frequency-response graphs. They should appear as close to flat line as possible

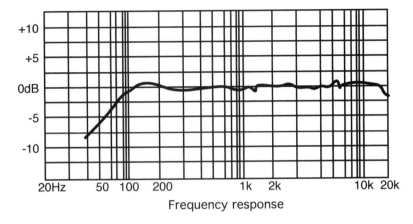

Frequency response

from 100Hz to over 15kHz. A higher dB might indicate that the louder speaker has a 4dB peak sticking up at 2kHz. So the speaker is louder due to a harsh peak, which can also cause feedback. That isn't good. We don't want to sacrifice quality for volume. If that were the case, stadium horns would be perfect. (In fact, I believe that's what they use in purgatory for the audiophile accommodations.)

Polar Response

PA speakers use horns to increase projection of high frequencies. Like a spotlight, horns *disperse* these frequencies in a narrower pattern with higher velocity to throw farther in a large room. Unfortunately, the sound can get messed up from bouncing around in the horn shell if the design doesn't perfectly complement the waveform created by the high-frequency driver on the back of the horn.

A polar response graph tells how good that design is. A great horn will show almost perfectly matched oval lines from 2kHz to 16kHz. A bad one will have all kinds of weird shapes. This represents frequencies that peak out at certain positions around the cabinet and drop out at others, changing your sound and level considerably throughout the room. Where the frequency-response curve tells how good the sound is directly in front of the cabinet, the polar response tells how good it is everywhere else! All this taken into account, a good speaker design can become pretty obvious.

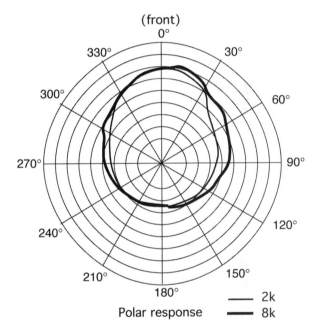

Polar response   —— 2k   —— 8k

CROSSING OVER

You might remember I skipped over **crossovers** in the signal processing section. Well, now it's time! These units help speakers do their job better and with less potential for damage. That's because they allow the various components to receive only the frequencies they're best suited for.

Full-range speakers have two or three components: a **woofer** for low frequencies, a **tweeter** (or driver) for high frequencies, and sometimes an additional **midrange** speaker dedicated to frequencies between the other two. Since the tweeter is very small compared to the woofer, it can't move enough to reproduce the lower frequencies and will be damaged by them. So the crossover filters out the low end going to the tweeter. Alternately, the woofer won't be damaged by high frequencies but does a sloppy job of reproducing the ones it can. So the crossover filters the highs from the low-frequency components. Similar concessions are made for a midrange driver, with its range usually somewhere between 500Hz and 5kHz.

Most full-range speakers have a non-powered **passive crossover** built in. This network takes the speaker signal coming in from the amplifier and does the filtering before it goes to the components in the cabinet. An **active crossover** is a powered unit that receives the line level signal from the mixer, then splits the frequencies *before* the amplifiers. Those split feeds then go to the individual amplifiers that power those specific ranges for the appropriate components. The advantages of this system are that crossover points are more precise and can be adjusted, independent levels can be set for

the various frequency ranges, and each amplifier can work a little easier doing a specific job.

As I mentioned in the previous chapter, some amplifiers include a simple built-in active crossover that can be switched on and adjusted for the appropriate crossover frequency. Digital signal processors also incorporate active crossovers with comprehensive control and output routing, and some speaker manufacturers make dedicated crossover/processors configured to work with their own specified enclosures. Active full-range speakers have also become popular, employing both active crossovers and amplifiers within the cabinet that are perfectly matched and tuned for the components.

In general, the quality of internal passive crossovers is okay for normal full-range speakers in portable sound and smaller venues. It's in larger systems and when using subwoofers that the active crossover becomes an essential addition, as we'll learn in a moment.

STUDIO MONITORS

In the recording studio, we need an accurate set of speakers since every move we make is based on what we hear. Unlike many home hi-fi speakers, which are designed more for subjective and cosmetic appeal, studio monitors are designed with *flat response* as a priority. The term implies "smooth and accurate," not "bland" like a carbonated drink gone bad. With an accurate reference, we will be able to mix recordings best-suited to all types of speakers that people may be listening to.

Studio monitors are usually two-way designs with woofers from 6–8 inches, or three-way with woofers of 10–15 inches. They'll typically use 1-inch dome tweeters and 3–5-inch midrange drivers, though some larger models employ horns. Popular manufacturers are JBL, KRK, Yamaha, M-Audio, Bag End, and Genelec. Tannoy and Urei offer models that use coaxial speakers, which employ a tweeter horn mounted in the middle of the woofer. **Active monitors** have built-in amps and active crossover to maximize the performance of the speaker. Though high-end models are understandably pricey, most are more economical than buying separate components, and they exhibit exceptional efficiency and sound quality. All the manufacturers above have active models available that include compatible subwoofers you can add to hear the lowest frequencies and know what's going on down there.

When choosing studio monitors, as with any speaker, the specs can tell us much of what we want to know, but listening will tell us the most. All good speakers sound a little different, and our preferences can be subjective, so pick one that appeals to you. And if you're not used to an accurate speaker, a good one will teach you a lot about how things should sound.

PA SPEAKERS

Full-range speakers typically use 10-inch to 15-inch woofers (though there are a few compact 8-inch and 5-inch designs for small spaces) and horn drivers of 1–3 inches, which is the size of the internal diaphragm, not the entire horn body. Most are two-way since current high-end drivers do such a good job through the upper ranges. Some cabinets use cheaper **piezo** horn/tweeters, which should be avoided in all but very minor applications. These elements are "beamy" and only reproduce above 6kHz, skipping right over the critical 2–5kHz vocal presence range. True **compression driver** horns offer wide dispersion and response as well as better power handling.

I've used narrower, dual 5–8-inch models in tight spaces, but generally use 12–15-inch single woofer designs for full-range speakers. I also consider it a mistake to buy larger *dual 15-inch* full-range with the idea that they will give you acceptable low-end performance. It is much better and similarly cost effective to keep the full-range compact and elevated to carry over the crowd, and add **subwoofer** cabinets, even single 15- or 18-inchers,

which are specifically made for efficient and powerful low end. It also makes 10–12-inch full-range more practical since they're not required to handle bass, and they reproduce the midrange better than a 15-inch woofer, along with less size, weight, and cost.

The powered PA enclosures I spoke of with crossover and amps built in can provide optimal performance with all components perfectly matched, as well as portable convenience for some people. It all depends on whether you prefer running just one cable (the speaker line) to each cabinet and carrying an amp rack separately, or having it all built in and running extra lines for both line signal and electrical power to each cabinet. Considering the extra weight in powered speakers and any potential for electronic failure, I lean more toward separate speakers and amps for installations. If a rack amp fails, I can simply switch to another one without the hassle of "uninstalling" a flying speaker and getting it repaired. You can make up your own mind as to whether powered speakers are more attractive in your application.

Waveguides & Line Array

These are two of the newer developments in PA horn design. The **circular** (or sometimes oval) **waveguide** is offered by a few companies, like WorxAudio, QSC, and Reinkus-Heinz. Since all high frequencies emanate in a spherical pattern from a *circular* driver, it makes sense to have a circular horn to best retain that sonic integrity and avoid the transformation problems of changing a circle to a square. (How did manufacturers lose sight of that fact?) In my experience, good waveguides have exhibited the best fidelity in conventional PA speakers and don't require any proprietary processing to achieve that. I personally believe most designs other than line array should be using circular waveguide horns. In fact, one of the developers of what many considered the best designs that evolved from the 1990s said to me, "Waveguides are it! The industry just doesn't get it yet."

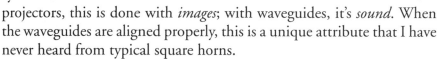

Though there is a wide choice of full-range designs for conventional horizontal (as opposed to vertical) arrays in small to medium room installations, circular waveguides offer some unique advantages: they tend to have a smoother and wider usable dispersion pattern from 60° to 90° without "beaminess," you can mount them in any rotated position with the same coverage, and the pattern is as high as it is wide for reaching first rows and balconies without supplemental speakers within their distance range. The better designs are also less prone to comb filtering, the screwy phase interaction you hear between speakers due to high-end overlap. This is because of the waveguide's smoother dropoff at the edge of its dispersion pattern, creating an audio effect similar to *edge blending* in multi-image projection. As the dispersion edge of one horn "feathers" away, the edge of the next horn overlaps with the same consistency to create a near-seamless transition between the two. With video projectors, this is done with *images*; with waveguides, it's *sound*. When the waveguides are aligned properly, this is a unique attribute that I have never heard from typical square horns.

Where conventional full-range are more economical for horizontal speaker arrays, for which the primary demand is width of coverage, **line arrays** offer much greater capability and control for depth of coverage. First introduced by L-Acoustics in their V-DOSC series at the end of the last century, line arrays have exploded on the market with variations by almost every major speaker manufacturer. The purpose here is multiple speakers that literally act as one. Put simply, the high-frequency horn is designed as a vertical slot that serves to meld as a near-continuous line through each cabinet, resulting in the most seamless high-frequency coverage. The vertical design and very wide coverage offered (as much as 140°) also cuts down on the number of arrays needed to cover a wide area, minimizing the comb filtering common to multiple speakers in a horizontal array.

Line-array enclosures have the most defined dispersion patterns, usually 120° horizontal by a mere 5°–15° vertical. This design allows a flexible arrangement of enclosures to accommodate the vertical coverage from front to rear seating in any venue, indoors or outdoors. If you need

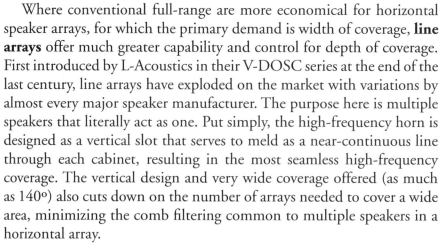

increased projection, you can have two or more enclosures aligned in parallel to work together for greater projection to the far distances. For instance, I could have two 5° designs on top pointing almost straight back to shoot 150 feet or more, three more in a progressively downward arc of 20° to cover the main floor up to 100

feet, and one 15° shorter throw on the bottom to catch the front rows. Brand-specific rigging hardware makes it easy to adjust the vertical angles of each speaker for optimal pattern control.

With their substantial width coverage, a single line array in a central cluster can often cover a whole room. If you need to cover more than a 120° width, you can fly two spaced line arrays or simply add conventional fills on each side. Full-size concert line-array enclosures can cost $5,000 or more each, run 4 feet long, and weigh almost 200 pounds, but there are smaller units available, like the Nexo Geo and JBL VTX series, to accommodate a wide variety of more modest rooms and outdoor areas. These include compact 8-inch or even 6.5-inch woofer designs that weigh less than 30 pounds each and cost less than half as much as the big boys. Nexo also provides a unique dispersion attachment that can change the width pattern from 120° to 80°, offering more coverage flexibility for multi-point systems or smaller areas.

Line-array manufacturers normally offer a digital processor specially designed for precise control, protection, and performance of the entire system. They may also combine amplification and processing in a single unit (like Nexo's powered TDControllers), or consolidate it as internal to their active enclosures. Though it all adds up to some expense, it's essential in applications that demand performance from the most unforgiving element of any sound package—the speakers.

Subwoofers

Subwoofers are usually single or dual 15-inch or 18-inch enclosures designed to maximize low-end output. I normally prefer dual 15-inch indoors for their naturally "tight" sound. Larger 18-inch subs can't turn around as fast and tend to sound a bit muddier indoors around the 80Hz range. Subs should be dedicated to ranges below 125Hz, depending on the system. I usually crossover subwoofers below 100Hz, and sometimes as low as 70Hz in smaller rooms for more "feel" and less "boominess" in close proximity to the cabinet. An active crossover either as a discrete component built in to amplifiers or

powered subs, or as part of a digital signal processor, will provide this deep range to the subwoofer and can filter low frequencies out of the full-range so they can work easier and sound clearer, too. The full-range can be elevated for better coverage, and the subwoofers left on the floor for maximum efficiency.

The reason for this efficiency is the omnidirectionality of low end. It uses planes, like a floor or wall, as an acoustic "amplifier" to increase efficiency in a room. In fact, I can get at least 6dB more bass and better distribution throughout most rooms by placing the sub on the floor and pointing it toward a wall, within 6 inches to a foot. While I may have four small suspended speakers, one or two subs placed to the rear or sides of the stage area facing a wall will provide broad low-end coverage throughout. Unless you're standing near them, you don't know where the low end is coming from. Most people just think the full-range speakers sound that good!

Spot Check

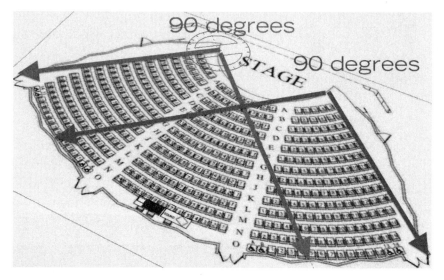

With any full-range speaker, particular attention should be given to the horn *dispersion*. Just as with mic pickup, we can direct our main speakers like spotlights to cover the necessary areas of the room. Plus, we want our stage mics to be out of their horn pattern to minimize feedback. A quick check is to put your wrists together and angle your palms out to form a right angle. Then point out toward the room and you can approximate the area a typical 90°-horizontal horn should cover. (You see, it's common sense, but even "professional" installers still mess up on coverage angles.) Speakers with 60–75° horns can throw more evenly over a longer distance, so use these when you need to project over 50 feet. Just narrow the palm angle slightly to spot-check.

Another concern is if you have to hit a balcony. You can adjust your palm angle sideways to get some idea of whether the typical 40° vertical pattern of a square horn will catch it. Circular waveguide horns make this easier because their pattern is 60–75° all around, and line arrays allow you to add and adjust speakers for more specific coverage. If a conventional speaker doesn't project high or far enough for a balcony, you need to add delayed speakers in front of the balcony areas or bite the bullet and invest in a line array system. (I'll talk about delayed speakers in a moment.)

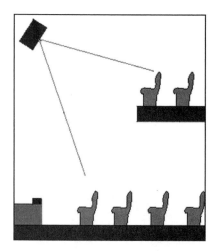

MONITORS

Stage Monitors

Monitor wedges are simply floor versions of our two-way full-range using 8-inch to 15-inch woofers. Horizontal horn coverage is important, so avoid wedges with the horn mounted vertically. (You don't need high end shooting up toward the ceiling.) Wider-coverage horns like waveguides can again offer broad coverage from side to side and forward and back. There are also smaller standmount designs, like the **Galaxy Hot Spot,** with one or two 5-inch speakers. Despite some audio critics, these are still useful for providing good mid/high

definition to one or two performers within a small space, and they also minimize excessive low end from the stage caused by larger, "bassier" floor monitors. You simply don't want a lot of bass piling up on stage. Any low end your performers can hear onstage from the main speakers will end up supplementing your stage monitors.

In-Ear Monitors

Though it strays slightly from our emphasis on *speakers* for the moment, it's important to address **in-ear monitoring (IEM)** in both multichannel and wireless versions. IEM can eliminate the amplifiers, cabling, stage monitor levels, and/or feedback of monitor speakers while offering a better mix that can potentially follow your artist to the ends of the Earth (if you can transmit that far). Like wireless mics, wireless IEMs use an audio transmitter and a receiver pack that normally operate in stereo on UHF frequencies. They utilize small earbuds that are inconspicuous and can block outside sound, and systems can run from around $1,000 to under $500 from companies like Shure, Sennheiser, and Galaxy. Some systems also have a "dual-mono" mode that allows you to switch the stereo feed to two mono feeds from a single transmitter, allowing you to select either mix on any receiver packs . . . a sort of two-for-the-price-of-one deal.

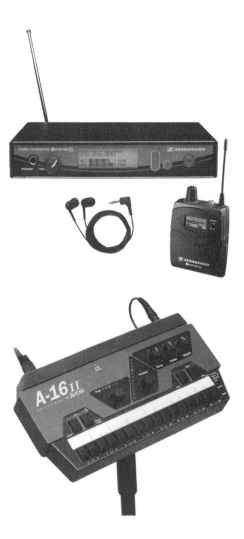

Companies like HearTechnologies, Aviom, and MyMix offer multichannel, wired, in-ear systems with significant advantages when you don't need to move around a lot. These systems handle 8 to 16 feeds from auxes, insert sends, or direct outs to their multichannel hub. The hub then converts the signals and sends them through Ethernet cables to individual remotes equipped with headphone outputs and separate controls for each channel, so everyone controls their own personal monitor mix. (Then a poor monitor mix won't be your fault anymore!) The remotes may include tone control, stereo panning, and mix memories. Aviom also offers a hub designed as an economical option card for Yamaha digital mixers.

Digital mixers are also incorporating their own versions of multichannel IEM via Ethernet, as with the Roland M48, Allen & Heath ME1, and Behringer P16 systems. Of course, these are proprietary systems unique to each mixer brand, so they are not compatible with each other. The manufacturers also offer tablet and smartphone apps to adjust mixer levels—they can control the monitor mix for a wireless IEM, but they don't transmit audio like an IEM.

The most important consideration for any multichannel IEMs is to send the right feeds for the performers to control. Normally I would send all the individual rhythm instruments and solo vocalists via pre-fader sends or direct outs from the main mixer. Drums are best split out for kick, snare, and hi-hat. Everything else can be grouped into single post-fader feeds, including the rest of the drum kit. This saves channels for control of the most essential items, and post-fader sends allow the main mixer's balance for grouped singers or choir, toms and cymbals, orchestra, etc. to be reflected in each of those IEM feeds.

Some monitoring options for these systems include hooking the earphone output of a multichannel IEM remote into a *wireless* IEM transmitter so you'll have both mix control and untethered movement. I've also patched to a powered monitor for a personal mix. With any IEM, be aware of the possibility of hearing damage if users aren't smart about adjusting their earphone levels, and take hygiene into account if earpieces are used by different people.

DELAY LINES

If you have seating out of the throw or line of sight of the main speakers (such as under a balcony or around a corner), it will require speakers dedicated to the area. Whether extra full-range or small ceiling speakers, they need to be on a high-quality **digital delay processor** (or a DSP unit with delay components) inserted before their amplifier to compensate for distances of 40 feet or more between the delayed speakers and the main speakers. Otherwise, you will have a noticeable echo between the two that blurs the sound. Digital mixers often have a built-in delay adjustment on their outputs, so no external delay unit will be needed.

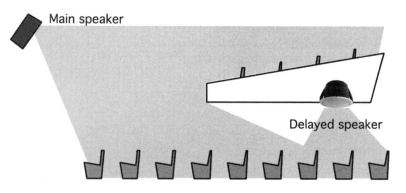

Main speaker

Delayed speaker

The delay time should be set at just under 1 millisecond per foot of distance between the main and delayed speakers, and some delays let you switch delay increments from milliseconds to simulated "feet." You can also tune it by ear with a well-defined rhythm source, such as drums on a soundtrack. While listening in the delayed area, have someone at the processor increase the delay time setting until you hear the echo disappear between the main and delayed speakers, and the rhythm hits occur simultaneously. From that point, increase the delay time another 5ms and the delayed speakers will almost seem to disappear. This is a result of the ***Haas effect*** mentioned in Chapter 7. When the room delay is set just a few milliseconds longer than needed, the ear is fooled into thinking the sound is coming from the original source. It's important, however, that the delayed system level and EQ be set to only supplement the mains as needed. Most of the time, a moderate level of mid/high definition is all that's required. Low and low-mid frequencies from the main speakers will usually reach or reflect into the delayed areas, adding fullness and supporting the *point-source reference*—that is, sound perceived to emanate from the direction of the stage. This is the intent of sound coming from speakers around the stage area in the first place. Using proper balance and the Haas effect for delayed systems can maintain this natural sense of direction.

If you have several rows of ceiling speakers for a deep underbalcony area, you may need to compromise the delay setting for the average depth, or incorporate a second delayed region farther back. A better choice here could be small, quality two-way speakers, with horns for better projection, mounted flush to the underbalcony ceiling near the front edge and facing back.

A dual 5-inch or other compact waveguide design with a wide-dispersion horn will excel here and will carry at least 30 feet. You just need enough speakers to string across the front of the underbalcony to cover the width necessary. For a deep area with a low ceiling height and a hard ceiling surface (or using similarly reflective drop-ceiling tiles), point each speaker straight back with no downward angle. This avoids blasting people closest to the speakers and helps reflect sound off the ceiling toward the rear seats. Think of it as playing billiards with audio, using horn dispersion and a hard surface to bounce the sound where you need it.

For the Record

RECORDING

Economical digital multitrack recorders preceded digital mixers by a few years in the early '90s and opened up a whole new world for the average musician and garage studio. Reel-to-reel tape recorders and even cassette multitracks (on the lowest end of the scale) served us well, but they were rendered obsolete by the quality, convenience, and expandability of new systems and software. Initially, digital had its own set of problems to overcome, but current products truly offer a level of performance previously unimagined in their price range. And just like digital mixers, they give us production potential that is still being expanded on today.

Advances in the technology continue to push the limits in audio as well as video recording and editing. But for legacy's sake, I'm going to offer a little history on the digital formats and features from the start of the 1990's explosion. Some of you may still have some older recorders in your arsenal or see them showing up as good buys on eBay. If nothing else, it's an interesting study of the ingenuity of manufacturers to satisfy the needs and creative potential of the masses.

RECORDERS

Professional 24-track analog recorders using 2-inch reel tape are still found in many studios. Like tube technology, analog has unique musical characteristics based on the subtle ways it captures sound rather than

its total perfection in reproducing it. But $25,000+ for a good machine, plus the cost of 2-inch tape at 30 IPS (over $100 for 15 minutes!), was prohibitive for the average musician's budget. Smaller 8-tracks with 1/2-inch tape and 16-tracks with 1-inch tape helped us poor engineers get through that analog era.

Now digital recorders and **workstations** (all-in-one multitrack production units like in the photo below) offer high-quality reproduction at much lower cost and unprecedented capabilities only possible in the digital realm. Though there's been a lot of argument over analog versus digital through the years, current technology, its track record, and the market has settled the matter. Personally, I welcome all that digital has to offer, and I've found ways to duplicate desired analog characteristics using creative miking, EQ, compression, and/or tube processing.

MDM Recorders

Modular **D**igital **M**ultitracks introduced by Alesis and Tascam used high-resolution **SVHS** or **Hi8** videotape to record digital audio. Adapting a digital format to economical and readily available video transports brought costs down to those previously associated with semi-pro tape machines, and advantages over those were numerous:

1. There was no inherent tape noise to contend with.
2. There was no need for sound-degrading noise reduction.
3. Spot editing (punch in/punch out) was totally seamless.
4. You could bounce or transfer tracks with no loss of quality.
5. Audio reproduction was consistent from machine to machine.
6. Synchronization of multiple machines was simple and much more accurate.
7. Complex functions were possible, such as digital routing and track delay.

MDMs functioned pretty much like a normal tape recorder, just with all the added capabilities. The only maintenance was periodic head cleaning, which was the same as for a video tape deck. Head life was estimated at 2,000 hours or more. Alesis ADAT recorders would even tell you how many actual hours of use were on the head.

A unique feature of MDMs was their inherent ability to synchronize together for more tracks. Big reel machines required expensive servomotors and synchronizers to lock together. MDMs needed only to loosely sync the motors; digital buffers made sure the audio was output precisely to timecode clocked at 48,000 times a second. This also made it much more cost-effective to manufacture a single 8-track model rather than divide production between 16- and 24-track models, too. Now you could just buy as many 8-tracks as you needed and lock them up. They could be synced to video or MIDI sequencing gear as well using available interfaces.

MDMs could be set to 48k or 44.1k sampling rate, the latter being the CD manufacturing standard. Recording time per tape varied from 40 to 100 minutes, depending on the machine. These unique inventions also demanded innovation for transferring eight digital tracks through a cable, so two new formats were devised: **ADAT optical** by Alesis and **TDIF multipin** by Tascam. ADAT optical became the more popular interface for later digital systems, including mixers, processors, and I/O option accessories.

Hard Disk Recorders

These multitrack units offer all the advantages of MDM tape systems plus more recording time and random-access location and editing capabilities. Like CDs, you can go to any point on your recording instantly, as well as copy, delete, and move things around. This is possible because information is being read off a computer hard disk as opposed to a linear piece of tape.

Though most multitrack systems are now software-based with a compatible computer, there have been standalone hardware systems with 16 to 24 tracks by Alesis, Mackie, Fostex, and Tascam. Some offered **waveform editing** as an integral or optional feature. As with software systems, this allows you to actually see the waveform on a screen, making it easier to creatively manipulate the audio: edit out noises or breath sounds, alter whole words, duplicate sections, etc. Loads of fun for the whole family!

You can also create different versions of a recording. Re-recording various sections to other locations is called the **copy** method. But another creative feature, called the **playlist,** allows you to designate different sections of a recording and simply program them to be played back in different arrangements without copying and using up more disk memory.

Hard disk recorders were usually more economical than a comparable computer-based system once you add up the software, a beefy computer, and the I/O interfacing needed to connect input sources and external gear. The older digital tape units were driven to extinction, and hard drive costs have plummeted while memory has soared from a mere 540MB in early units to a terabyte now for under $100. That's over 100 hours of 24-track recording!

MiniDisc (or MD) Recorders

The Sony MiniDisc format was successfully exploited in the multitrack market for a time with 4-track and 8-track units by Sony, Yamaha, and Tascam. The MDs offered many of the advantages of hard disk but on a cost-effective and removable MD Data Disc, which held about 140 minutes total time and, unlike CDs and DVDs, was shielded in a protective "floppy disk"-style shell. They also proved useful for live production soundtracks in theatre, with instant cueing like CDs, song titling, and extra tracks for adding voiceovers, sound effects, and overlapping song transitions. MDs used a proprietary data-compression scheme, so they were never employed as a "full-quality" professional format.

Magneto-Optical (MO) Recorders

MO was a promising format that got lost in the transitional shuffle of new technologies, falling somewhere between a recordable CD and a MiniDisc: random access, re-recordable, housed in a casing (like MD), available in 3.5-inch and 5-inch versions, and recording uncompressed audio. Though first introduced by Akai with their DD1000 2-track, it surfaced again in short-lived modular 8-track models by HHB and

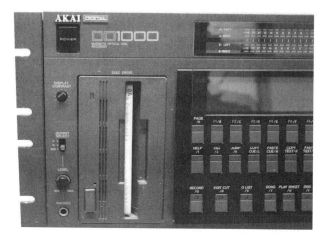

Yamaha. Everything you always wanted in a MiniDisc . . . and more. I wouldn't mind seeing an economical version of the MO media revived as an encased DVD and/or Blu-ray "Pro" format protected from scratches by a shell. How about it media manufacturers?

DAT Recorders

Digital Audio Tape recorders were actually the first affordable digital format available in the late '80s. Originally designed as a consumer product, it was soon clear that consumers wouldn't take the higher-cost bait, so DATs ended up being adopted by the pro audio industry as a standard mastering format for cassette and CD manufacture as well as for archiving. DATs recorded stereo digital audio on special tapes sharing a single data track, so they were not capable of punch in/out editing or recording separate tracks. Though subject to the normal wear of tape and mechanics, they established their reliability over the years. There were even a few portable "Walkman-type" models, like my Casio DA-R100, which I could sneak into concerts or presidential Cabinet meetings. It had a stereo mic/ line input, digital coaxial, and optical connections, and you could set ID points like a CD. (I still have that old DA-R100 that's as small as a guitar pedal, and it still works!)

DATs would record up to 120 minutes of audio at 48kHz (better than CD) or 44.1kHz standards, and some had the capability of 32kHz "nonlinear" long-play recording for up to 4 hours. This limited frequency response to about 15kHz, but it was great for long programs, lectures, and saving my old vinyl albums . . . scratches and all.

CD Recorders (CDR)

I'm sure you're acquainted with CDRs, but it was really only since the late 1990s that we had affordable, recordable, wish-we'd-had-'em-before-dable CD recorders. Three formats have been available: the **RedBook** (pro-format) **CDR,** which records audio or data on standard blank CDs, and for consumer recorders, **Digital Audio CDR,** which records only audio (no files or graphics), and **CDRW,** which records on rewritable CDs. The reason for the latter two was to give record companies a little dividend from sales due to obvious home copying, plus protection from mass-population pirating. Consumer CDR(W) recorders were cheaper, but they incorporated "copy prohibit" in the format to prevent direct digital copies from being made.

When we finally had the luxury of mix automation with some digital mixers, I switched to CD for my mastering medium. Before affordable automation, we were destined to make numerous attempts at the final mix, trying to get all those knob and fader moves just right. Since write-once pro CDRs could not be re-recorded after a mistake, re-recordable DAT or hard drive mastering was our logical choice. But then automation became the master! All settings and moves are recorded in the mix software so you just start the CDR, hit the Automix button, and a perfect mix is transferred while you sit back and enjoy your prune juice. Some multitrack workstations, like the Yamaha AW4416, had it all: the digital mixer with mix automation, 16-track recorder with an extra stereo track for mixdown, and a built-in CDR for mastering and data storage.

MP3

I can't conclude digital recording without mentioning iPods and MP3. A few decades ago, you had a portable radio that you carried around, and then a cassette player, and then a CD Walkman, but they all lacked greater selection and quantity. Now you can live in your own universe devoid of the world around you with thousands of songs streaming from your pocket into your earbuds. (Is that a good thing?) This was made possible by the MP3 recording format, which condensed stereo audio down to one-tenth the size of uncompressed CD audio.

Though not a pro format because of the compression scheme (which does affect the sound quality), it certainly is the best combination of quality *and* quantity to come along, and it has made it possible to have internet access to an unlimited catalogue of songs. Just don't let it render you an unproductive member of society or mislead you into plundering the investment and hard work of the music makers. They need to eat, too.

It probably won't be long for the newest products to make it into the Smithsonian, with all the continuous advances in digital technology. One of my hopes is that all digital equipment will eventually adopt compatible standards to fully integrate and communicate. The near future should spawn more surprises in the field, googlabytes of random-access memory (RAM), and maybe even dilithium-crystal recording with warp drives! Stardate . . . sooner than you think.

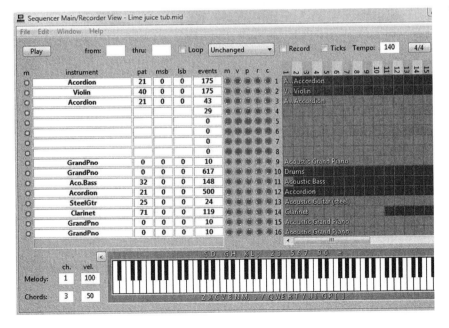

VIRTUAL TRACKING

One more recording note: If you have keyboards, sound modules, drum machines, or sound software with MIDI sequencing capability, you already have another type of "digital recording" system. Sequencing records musical "tracks" as you play the above equipment, then automatically triggers all those notes and parts on the same equipment as a complete arrangement. You can synchronize the MIDI clock to hardware or software multitrack recorders to have both tracks and sequences play together in perfect time. This is called **MIDI**

sync, and we even used to do it with analog tape multitracks using a tape-to-sync interface, like the J.L. Cooper PPS-2. With most digital systems, MIDI sync can work in both directions—either sequencer as master and multitrack as slave, or vice versa—and it will tell the slave when and where to start and how fast to go.

Suddenly, all your sequenced outputs become additional live tracks playing along with your multitrack system. You won't need to record these parts and use up tracks; you can make quick changes at any time by simply editing your sequences, and any keyboards or modules you add become more MIDI tracks. All you need is additional mixer channels to handle the extra outputs which, it so happens, are available or expandable on most digital mixers and workstations.

Audio By Design

12

IT'S TIME I CONFESSED SOMETHING, AND IT WILL PROBABLY blow any semblance of wisdom I've attempted to build to this point . . . I once bought a used 1987 Hyundai. There, I said it, but let me explain. I didn't know they were pretty lame back then. (But they learned from experience and now make great cars!) I got a good deal. (Obviously.) It looked to be in great shape. (Okay, I wasn't wearing my glasses.) Everything seemed mechanically sound. (So now I'm an automotive expert.) And the thing turned out to be a disaster on wheels.

Somehow I missed the point. While ignorantly considering its apparent outward appearance, I overlooked a more important point . . . something having to do with *motion*. The same thing can happen with audio. You need to have a concept of what you're trying to accomplish, or you'll go nowhere. All the fancy tools are worthless without realistic goals and skills. I hope to start you on a basic blueprint in this section.

RECORDING

The studio is the most controlled and critical audio environment, making it a great spot to sharpen your skills, train your ears, and experiment with ideas. Unlike live sound situations, there are few background noises and room reflections to mask the audio details you need to hear, you have the luxury of being able to do "one more take" until you get it the way you want it, and you have an excellent reference on which to base your results—national quality recordings. You can listen to them side by side with your projects to make immediate comparisons and corrections.

If things sound too good to be true, they are. There is an inherent problem with recording that the uninitiated fail to consider. In a live performance, you have sound arriving at your ears from a multitude of sources and directions. Each ear receives its own sound waves with all kinds of complex location information to help separate and clarify the different components and direction of the sounds.

In *stereo* production, all this needs to be duplicated by two speakers, two positions. A lot of critical information is missing, limiting the ear's ability to distinguish the sources and their placement clearly. So we must compensate somehow to help simulate (and stimulate) the "transparency" of the natural environment. This is done with what I call "**The Five P's of Production**."

Frequency Pockets

Vocals, guitars, keyboards, bass, horns, drums . . . all this conglomeration gets jammed through speakers, and suddenly it's like a small room crowded with people. They're stepping on each other's toes, and it's hard to see who's who. If we can dress them all in different-colored clothes and spread them out more, maybe we can improve the perspective.

In mixing, the different instruments can quickly start muddling together, especially in the lower frequencies, where bass starts piling up. *My first fix is to roll bass EQ out of non-bass sources.* Voices, guitars, horns, most keyboard parts, etc. don't need much if any low end below 100Hz. What *is* there will usually get in the way of bass and kick drum and destroy clarifying contrast between low- and high-end sounds. So take it out on appropriate channels to the point where the sound clears up, but before it gets too thin.

Next, we'll start identifying and dedicating the frequency ranges where our individual instruments best fit. For example, kick drum "feel" is concentrated around 50–63Hz, with high-end punch around 3kHz, so maybe I'll EQ the bass guitar to accent the 63–200Hz range with definition up to 2kHz. Keyboards can provide warmth and body through the 200–600Hz range, with highs up to 6kHz, so I'll EQ the lead guitar to stand out in the 500–800Hz range with some bite at 2kHz. I could also take frequencies above 4kHz out of guitar to better simulate the response of a 12-inch speaker cabinet and to make room for the high-end "brilliance" of vocals and cymbals. Sax will fit nicely in the 700Hz–5kHz spot, and vocals, with their slightly higher levels, should predominate from 400Hz to 12kHz. Cymbals and some percussion will top everything off with sweet highs up over 10kHz.

Though these are only examples, and other frequencies are present in all these instruments, giving each its own special "pocket" makes each more discernible and evens out levels throughout the frequency spectrum. In fact, with a **real-time analyzer** hooked up (even as a smartphone app), you can listen to instruments one at a time and get some visual indication of where each is in the mix, and then experiment with getting a smoother response on your recordings. As I discussed in the section on equalizers, most of this is accomplished by cutting back nonessential frequencies rather than by boosting the desired ones. This takes a bit of work and lends itself to the next important aspect of mixing.

Priorities (also known as Commitment)

No room for "wishy-washy" Charlie Browns here. When I use creative EQ to improve overall balance and separation, I also commit to sonic elements that listeners may be able to identify and relate to. And I can choose to be conspicuously different or even radical in this endeavor, attracting attention to the music and its components.

Such easily recognizable aspects of a song, in composition or production, are called **hooks**. The more good ones you have, the more likely the song will be noticed. The same concept applies to instrument balance. Everybody can't be the "star." *Pick the strongest and most dominant themes and commit those out front.* Mix the rest comfortably in the background bed to create a good foundation of support. If there isn't a dominant, memorable theme, *create one!* Don't just jam up a bunch of weak ideas. The song is only as strong as its weakest link.

Sometimes it may seem hard to keep priorities like vocals from getting enveloped by other sounds. The trick is using pockets along with keeping the denser instruments lower in the mix. You may need to EQ down the over-2kHz range on keyboards or distortion guitar to make more room for vocal presence. I often prefer to get more power out of my mixes by kicking the drums a little stronger, since they offer a lot of open spaces for the vocals to come through. Then my rhythm instruments can *collectively* equal the level of the drums. Bass is adjusted to complement the kick drum (or vice versa) and add fullness to the overall mix. Finally, I'll ride the leads and instrumental hooks, bringing them up and down to fill in gaps between vocal parts.

Be aware of the tendency for multiple vocals coming in together to exceed a desired overall level. When that happens, the music starts sounding weak. When harmony parts come in, don't bring them up to the lead. Rather, have them set at least 3dB lower and blend the lead back into them for those parts, maintaining a more consistent overall level and avoiding peaks.

Panning

We'll use the stereo channel pans to move things left and right in the mix and create a two-dimensional image. I designate settings as clock positions: 9:00, 2:00, 12:00, etc. Except for actual stereo tracks such as keyboards, effects, or stereo mic pairs, I usually don't pan sources full left or right. It can sound like one ear is stopped up if you're wearing headphones.

I also give a lot of consideration to panning sources with similar characteristics to opposite sides for better balance and separation. If the hi-hat is panned right, the high-end-percussive acoustic guitar is left. If sax is left, lead guitar is right. Sopranos right, altos left, and so on. Pan everything a little differently to maximize separation, and make sure your left/right metering maintains a relatively even balance. This also means that strong low-end sources such as bass and kick drum should remain centered.

Perspective

Mic technique can be a crucial aspect in creating a three-dimensional perspective. ***Stereo miking*** is one of the most effective because it captures natural room characteristics recognizable to our ears. The better the room ambience, the better the effect. And using this technique for recording background vocalists or other multiple sources all together provides the imaging of each element being in a unique position in the mix.

When close-miking a single source, you could record another mic strategically placed back in the room to pick up the ambience. Pan the two toward opposite sides in the mix and you get a nice natural effect.

Try using ***phase reverse*** on some channels at mixdown if you have it available. This is a feature on digital and high-end analog consoles that is used to switch the polarity of the source signal. I've used it a few times on a background vocal, cymbals, and high-end percussion when it offered a slight change in front-to-back perspective in the mix. Don't use it on the major elements, on low-end stuff, or on half of a stereo source since it will cause phase cancellation.

Of course, there have been a few black boxes for simulated 3-D through stereo speakers, but we must assume that most won't sound the same on other speakers and headphones. Used discreetly, some 3-D processors, like the earlier **Hughes Retriever,** have given me nice results on specific stereo tracks, such as drum overheads, background vocals, and stereo effects, pulling them out into a nice 3-D field. If you get a chance, you might experiment with the potential of these devices if there are any still around. You may come up with your own sound and special effects.

Processing

Digital effects are the second stage of developing our three-dimensional image, with ***reverbs*** being the most common addition. They simulate the space of a variety of rooms. An easy way to make a source sound more distant is to roll off EQ above 4kHz and add more reverb, simulating the added ambience and loss of high end over distance. Another technique I use is recording a lead vocal twice, then mixing the first dry and the second as *full* stereo reverb (no original signal) subtly blended in. The slight timing differences between the two make for a deeper, more dimensional sound. You can also set reverb **pre-delay** for an intended room depth, say a rough setting of 60ms for 60 feet. (Some delays let you switch delay increments from milliseconds to simulated "feet.")

Along with some additional notes in Chapter 7, "Cause & Effect," there are endless possibilities that you'll just have to jump in and explore.

LIVE RECORDING

I've known people who wanted to have the capability of multitrack recording and live mixing simultaneously. The problem with using direct and group outs from a live analog console to the multitrack is that any channel EQ or level adjustments for the house mix are going to be printed to tracks, and they may not be constructive. A digital console offers more flexibility here, with a lot of routing options on its digital outputs, including pre-fader and even pre-EQ direct outs.

A useful approach for portable recording with various analog mixers is to invest in some 8-channel rackmount mic preamps, three of which can feed 24 tracks in only three rack spaces. Just send mic lines through these to the multitrack, set levels with enough headroom at the sound check, and let it roll. Either a split snake or the multitrack outputs (set to Input mode) can be fed to the live console, and a totally independent mix for the house can be achieved. Another option is using the mixer channel inserts as pre-fader sends to the recorder (discussed on page 34) if distance is kept short, since lines will be unbalanced. Unlike direct outs, inserts are normally pre-EQ so that EQ changes on the house mix will not affect recording.

As I briefly mentioned in Chapter 2, orchestral recording can be accomplished with just a quality **_stereo pair_** in the hall. With multitrack capability, however, we have the luxury of section miking to give us more mix control. One concern of mine, if multitracking in conjunction with the stereo pair, is the potential distance and delay between the hall mics and any section mics. One solution is to use the high-resolution channel **_delay_** available in digital mixers. In the mixdown, we can delay those individual section tracks to match the distance of the hall mics, achieving a perfect combination of natural stereo sound along with intimate instrumental detail and balance. In other words, you can have your cake and eat it too!

If you're just doing a stereo feed straight off the main mixer outputs, you may find your record mix balance a little off. The live mix is a calculated blend of system and ambient sound, with the softer elements like vocals and violins reinforced more, the louder elements like brass and percussion reinforced less. By contrast, the recorder sees only the system signal, which may result in soft stuff blasting and loud stuff getting lost in the background. The smaller the room, the more pronounced the inconsistency. It's best to use dual or stereo post-fader aux sends so compensated level adjustments can be made to the individual channels, creating a custom balance of your mix for stereo recording. Digital mixers make this even better by providing aux pans when two sends are in *stereo-pair* mode.

Final Notes: Here are some last-minute tips before you fall into the piteous pit of perpetual production pursuits:

- Always get good levels to tracks, even with digital. It improves digital resolution and will aid console signal-to-noise.
- Don't overdo low end! If you have to hear a 9dB boost below 60Hz, crank up subwoofers. Don't try to cram it on tracks and eat up your dynamic range.
- Use compressors conservatively for the fewest side effects. If you wish to mildly limit the whole mix, use a quality tube or digital processor for best results.
- When recording a drum set, get at least one minute of just toms and cymbals at the head of the tracks. This will make it easier to get mixdown settings on them, since they are usually sparse in the music itself.

- If you're lacking in effects units, print the less ambient ones to tracks like chorus, pitch shift, etc. Save dimensional reverbs and delays for the final mix.
- Always double-check your final mixes at low volume levels, where your ears become a "mid-reference." Listen for overall balance, making sure the instruments don't get wimpy in relation to the vocals. Everything should still be distinct.
- Always commend any producer on how lovely he/she looks today.

LIVE SOUND

I chose to cover recording first, because most of its aspects will carry over beautifully here. Obviously, studio-quality sound would be optimal, but it is difficult to achieve due to the nature of this "uncontrolled" environment. (This implies that you will be forced to adapt to the characteristics of the many rooms you may be working in.) Fortunately, the energy and visual stimulation of a live performance help mask many of the subtle flaws and add to the overall impact of the sound, but you'll still have to deal with room acoustics, stage volume, background noise, speaker tuning, level and coverage requirements, and hecklers demanding Lynyrd Skynyrd and Aerosmith. And that's just in a Christian concert!

High wattage and levels are major concerns here. The whole idea of a live performance is often to be conspicuous and dynamic, and this must be maintained over any competing levels from enthusiastic crowd response. Unfortunately, many groups try to squeeze too much out of an inadequate system. If you have quality speakers well-matched to amplification, system gain set up properly, mixer meters hitting at **unity gain**, and you still don't have enough level, you need more speakers and amps. Simple. *Save up!*

In live sound, I may find myself pushing 60Hz in the kick and bass a little hotter to increase "punch" and perceived level without resorting to excessive high frequencies that can damage hearing. I'll make up headroom with **subsonic filtering**, taking out frequencies below 40Hz on my master EQ or Low Cut control. This tightens up the bottom end and saves wattage. Depending on the room and speakers, I may also add a touch more above 5kHz to carry brilliance in vocals.

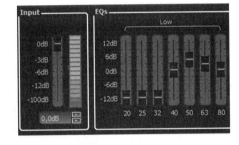

When you're hooking up your system, also be aware of the current draw of all your amplifiers. It is usually listed on the back of the amps by the AC cord or fuse. It's listed in amperes, such as "12A." If they only show *electrical wattage* (not the speaker wattage), use the formula WATTAGE ÷ 110 = AMPERES. (The 110 is the voltage off the wall.) You need to know this so you don't overload the electrical wall circuits, most of which are only 15–20A for each duplex pair. Unless you're equipped for high-power taps, request and use 20A circuits if available, and divide up amps to different circuits as necessary. Be aware of the potential for ground loops if you do. The good news is that some newer amps, like the Yamaha EEE designs, draw as little as half the current of previous models. You should check these specs if you anticipate power limitations.

The Few Less P's of Performance Production

Why less? Because we aren't concerned with perspective; the live room creates that. Even *processing* is applied more as special effect, since rooms will define their own ambience. The other three P's take on some unique perspectives.

Frequency pockets can be an advantage here, too. They help in the studio due to the limitations of speaker reproduction. In the live venue, they can help offset the cluttering nature of room acoustics. You will also find your equalizing based on the combination of live and electronic sound. If the sound of the instrument amps and stage monitors produce a lot of low and low-mid in the room, you will be more conservative in this area through the main system and potentially concentrate more on EQ above 500Hz.

Priorities need to be maintained and are often in competition with stage levels. Use creative ideas to limit these levels in smaller venues. When instrument amps are miked, coax the performers to face them across stage or rearward like stage monitors, or use a baffle to block sound shooting at the audience and run their volumes at the lowest acceptable levels. (They can supplement through wedges or IEMs.) Use a Clearsonic drum shield at least 5 feet high around drums if needed, and place some freestanding sound-absorbing baffles behind the drums to keep additional sound from bouncing off hard back walls. Use your ear, or analyzer, to determine which lower frequencies from the stage monitors are most pronounced in the room and drop these another 3–6dB on the monitor graphic to reduce that resonance. Most of the time, I choose to EQ everything below 100Hz out of the monitors. This reduces excessive bass buildup on stage and in the room and gives the monitor system more headroom. All this can greatly improve your control of the mix out front.

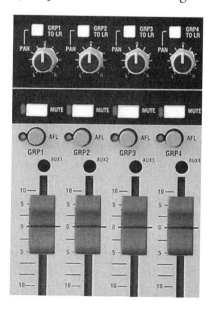

Panning brings up another aspect of live sound—whether you should run a monaural or stereo system. Mono is more typical, though it may be just as economical to run stereo, and with minor advantages. The house signal is divided between two output buses (Left and Right), increasing overall headroom through the system, and some stereo sources, such as keyboards, digital effects, or soundtracks, may have a richer, cleaner sound when their imaging is maintained. You just don't want to pan mono sources so that people sitting on the left side miss the stuff you panned toward the right. Remember that the majority of the audience will not be sitting in the sweet spot where stereo has its worthwhile effect.

Systems usually run mono when the operator needs to *group* channels on an analog mixer. On four- or eight-group consoles, the pans are used in conjunction with the assign switches to physically route multiple channels out a common group fader for easy submaster control. Then those group faders are fed to the main outs. Since all the channels sent to one group are routed through a single group fader, it will be mono. For something like stereo keyboard, you would have to assign it to two group faders panned in stereo, which uses up available groups twice as fast. A way around this is to route any stereo stuff directly to the main L/R outs. All the other mono stuff can be grouped as needed.

As discussed earlier, VCAs, DCAs, and digital fader groups don't have this limitation. Since their channel groups are created by either linking the motorized faders of the channels or assigning them to *remote control* faders that directly adjust channel levels, no physical routing is necessary. Each channel is free to pan, allowing you to group and maintain full stereo flexibility when needed. I use panning for some other live purposes as well, which I'll touch on under Church Sound in this chapter.

Monitors

A smooth sound through the 500Hz to 5kHz range with good definition at 2–3kHz is important to clarity that can cut through stage levels. Don't try to blast everything; the sound will just get loud and cluttered and nobody will be happy. Compromise with the performers on balancing the most crucial parts that need to be heard. If levels start getting out of hand or close to feedback, start backing out or removing the less important stuff to accentuate the priorities and clean up the sound. Roll out low end on the monitor EQs to reduce muddiness. (There will generally be plenty of low-end support from the main system.) Small monitors, like Galaxy Hot Spots or 10-inch two-ways, can help minimize sound bleed and stage level, while multichannel and wireless in-ear monitor systems can eliminate it all together.

Feedback

The best defense against feedback is a well-tuned system, hypercardioid mics, and staying within the capabilities of your system and environment. If a consistent feedback area occurs in mains or monitors, locate the one or two sliders on their graphic EQ that affect it most and lower those only slightly. There are typically only two or three spots that need control. Beyond that, you will find yourself progressively dropping all your sliders in a snowball effect, losing gain and quality. (More in Feedback Control shortly.) Again, use a real-time analyzer to help find feedback points. Even smartphone apps like Spectrum Analyzer or FrequenSee are good enough to direct you to the problem. As a last resort, especially on the road, when you may have little time to get through the setup process, a feedback suppressor like a Sabine FBX or DBX Pro AFS unit is designed to automatically find and remove it.

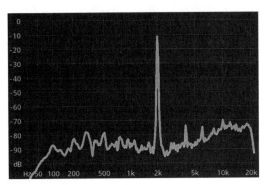

CHURCH SOUND

The church audio environment is almost a contradiction, just like *sound engineer*. (That's *sound* as in "sane, rational, responsible, wise, perceptive, logical, sober!" I rest my case.) That's because church audio incorporates sophisticated audio systems for public speaking, music production, concerts, theatrical presentations, and recording. And who typically runs it all? Volunteers!

On top of that, we have a very discerning and broad audience of 1- to 100-year-olds who aren't concerned with technicalities. They just want things to sound good and look nice. I can't think of a more complex situation to be in, unless you're a pastor who has a poor sound system. Then prayer is the first step. This section is the second.

Sanctuary Studios

I use the term sanctuary *studios* because church audio is more of a controlled environment. Once things are set up properly in your room, procedure and operation can be pretty consistent from week to week with few changes except for special presentations. Major emphasis should be on logical system design for ease of use, equipment and settings labeled and logged (and stored on digital equipment) as a constant reference, and one person dedicated to overseeing operations and related decisions. Too many cooks spoil the broth.

In addition, a well-tuned speaker system will give you an accurate reference (as reference monitors do in the studio), allowing you to make proper EQ and balance decisions that transfer favorably to any recording or broadcast applications you may employ. Thankfully, ministries that have contemporary worship are also giving more attention to acoustical design and/or absorption in their sanctuaries to help control volume and reflections. If they're not, remind them, since it is crucial to the overall sound.

Speakers

Speaker choices and configurations are of prime importance. I've seen cheap *and* expensive setups that sounded terrible and only covered half the sanctuary. Obviously, the salesmen or installers didn't have a clue or didn't care. (They may have claimed to be nondenominational, but I'll bet they favored $50s and $100s.)

Line arrays offer the most defined and adjustable patterns, coverage, and projection for larger venues, but I would leave these complex systems to professional installers. For conventional (side-by-side) center arrays, I suggest two-way speakers with a horizontal horn **dispersion** of 60° to 75°, since these will throw more evenly over distance than a 90°. (*No piezo horns!* Refer to Chapter 10 for more guidance.) Horns should be directed toward the rear seating of the sanctuary, with the lower, forward edge of the horn pattern catching the first row.

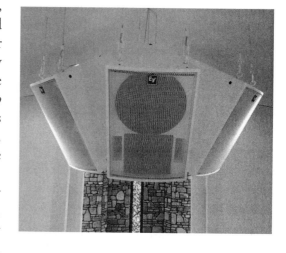

Speakers with 12-inch woofers (or potentially 10-inch for the smallest rooms) offer better vocal clarity than 15-inch, along with lighter weight, smaller size, and lower cost. Any speakers elevated in a *free field* (no boundaries nearby) will lack sub-bass anyway, so add a subwoofer somewhere on the floor or under the staging for more efficiency. If it's a smaller room (no more than 60 feet wide) and speakers are mounted on each side or placed in side

chambers (like those for organ speakers), 15-inch two-ways without subs may be sufficient due to increased bass efficiency from being close to walls or boundaries. When the placement is appropriate, chambers can also offer easier access for maintenance and a less conspicuous location.

Another consideration is how *sound energy* is concentrated or distributed. A center cluster is best if hung around 20 feet or more above the stage. If it hangs at only 10–12 feet because of a low ceiling, all the sound energy will be closely concentrated over some of the more feedback-prone mics, namely the pastor's wireless and the podium mic. Side placement may then be best, splitting the speakers to each side and as high as possible so the sound energy is distributed over a wider field, reducing the feedback potential at any particular spot on stage. Even if the pastor is standing on the far-side floor in front of a speaker, he is only close to half the energy. Also, with smaller rooms, you don't have to be overly concerned with point-source reference because the ambient sound of most vocals and instruments will carry enough. The speakers merely offer supplemental level and definition.

Though a center array can be a safe bet in many rooms, I find multipoint configurations better or even necessary in a lot of medium to large facilities due to a trend toward wider arced or arena-style rooms and stronger music programs. One approach is a conventional **spaced array,** where matching speakers are elevated and spread out around an arced stage, each covering its own area or seating section. Their dispersion pattern needs to be carefully chosen and positioned to provide even coverage all the way around with minimal overlap and no dropouts. I also discovered that there were more creative approaches to system design beyond the norm. One such approach is what I call *acoustic emulation.* In other words, if individual instruments and vocals can acoustically exhibit location and timing differences in a three-dimensional field, why can't speakers serve to emulate that? With this in mind . . .

Cluster, LCR & CS

While road engineers envision line arrays or speaker stacks on each side of the stage, the **center cluster** can be expanded to offer unique advantages in sanctuaries or theaters. Its primary purpose is to provide a central *point-source reference,* meaning sound is naturally coming from the direction of the primary action—namely pastors and performers at center stage.

Combining a center cluster with side speakers will create another multipoint system. When such a setup is configured to provide the same signal to all speakers for extended coverage of a very wide or oddly shaped room (similar to a spaced array), that's a **center cluster with side fills.** When it is designed to send discrete signals to Left, Center, and Right speakers via three mixer outputs, that's an **LCR** system. Some manufacturers have designed mixing consoles specifically for Left, Center, and Right main outputs, but a "pseudo" LCR setup can be accomplished with almost any stereo mixer. One way is to use the stereo out for L-R and a group, matrix, or mono output for Center. But a more practical approach is to forget about running stereo, which isn't necessary in most live applications because few people are in the sweet center spot to get any benefit. Instead, you can run the Left output to Center and the Right output to Left-Right speakers in mono. With this **CS** (**C**enter-**S**ides) setup, the channel pan control determines whether a source comes through the center (panned left), sides (panned right), or anywhere in between.

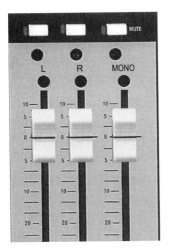

The initial idea of true Left-Center-Right was to maintain more accurate direction of three-point sound consistent with performers' positions on stage, but a more substantial benefit is to promote better separation between the vocals and the instruments. I often install this CS setup in churches and theaters with the center cluster speakers dedicated to vocals, and the side speakers—positioned a little farther back than the center cluster for a slightly different timing perspective—dedicated to instruments and soundtracks. The quality of sound is significantly improved because vocals and instruments aren't competing with each other through the same speakers in the same dimensional plane. It also provides a clarifying variance in sound distribution that emulates natural acoustics recognizable to our ears: a musical group behind and surrounding the front and center vocalists. This is my typical setup for *acoustic emulation*.

With the Left-Right to Center-Sides setup, for example, I can pan the actors, pastors, and lead vocalists full left to the center cluster. Most stage instruments can pan full right to the sides. I would pan soundtracks just slightly to the left to fill in a center gap, since they don't have any ambient direction from the stage the way instruments do. (If it's a split track, I can conveniently pan the vocal channel to the cluster and music channel to the sides.) If the primary instrument is piano or acoustic guitar, I can pan that more toward the left, where it's more out front. Background vocals can be panned slightly to the right to make them a little wider and move them behind the lead, and choir channels can have their pans centered so they come equally through cluster and sides, making them broad and deep, like a choir actually is! This gives you some idea of the creative and dimensional potential of a CS system.

I usually use 15-inch two-way side speakers for the music and 12-inch center speakers for better vocal definition. If you have subwoofers, you can opt for 12-inch full-range for the sides and configure the subs with them. (You don't need subs for the vocal cluster.) As a final note, it's important that the center cluster and side speakers in a CS system each be positioned to perform as two full-coverage systems since they are doing individual jobs. In general terms, the center cluster must cover the whole room for vocals, and the side speakers must collectively cover the whole room for music. Of course, if the room is too wide for full coverage from a center vocal cluster, then you're back to a mono spaced array or center cluster with side fills.

(Note: Always make sure elevated speakers are properly suspended and equipped with safety-approved stand mount or hanging hardware.)

Another way I have used creative L-R routing for ease and flexibility with mono sound systems is to use the Left output for the full-range mains and the Right output for subwoofers. Now I don't have to worry as much about sub low-end on vocal mics or rhythm instruments. I can pan the kick, bass, maybe keyboards, and soundtracks to center for both full-range and subs. Everything else pans full left for full-range only. It's easy routing and assures your channel fader moves will maintain the proper balance between the two systems.

Though I encourage you to consult with a professional on speaker system design, I can offer a few of my personal guidelines:

- *Side mounting*: rooms with lower ceilings, and no more than 60 feet wide with center aisle (minimizes audible phase cancellation). Speakers should be 10–15 feet high, and at least 10 feet back from the first row of seats. Will also cover most balconies.
- *Cluster*: rooms with ceilings 20 feet or higher, more than 60 feet wide, or those without center aisle or side placement locations. Centered over pulpit, use two speakers arrayed to cover 100° to 120°, three or four for arc seating requiring wider coverage. Horns should be at least 15–20 feet high, depending on depth of room and possible balcony coverage.
- *Multipoint*: a combination of the previous two, either as CS or side fill, for larger rooms or those wider than they are deep. (Can also be used when lower ceilings demand that sound be supplemented through side speakers to distribute sound energy.)

Rooms seating over 1,000, those with unusual acoustics (I once evaluated a sanctuary that had so many reflections arriving simultaneously at one spot, it created its own pitch!), or complex balcony or side-wing construction will require more strategic design. These will require line array or a combination of cluster, side fills, and delayed-speaker arrangements. Leave it to the professionals unless you're really brave and the church is very forgiving.

Apart from normal stage wedge, IEM, and multichannel monitoring, churches often need to provide monitors for choir or a large ensemble. You need these monitors elevated and focused on the choir area.

Any placed on the floor will be blocked by the first row from getting to the back rows. Monitors installed at ceiling heights above 15 feet will be too far from the choir, prompting a need for more level and causing excessive sound bouncing around the stage.

My choice whenever possible is to provide a good monitor to each side of the choir, no more than 10 feet from the closest person, and elevated with the horn at a height about even with the last row of singers. This allows them to be close to the choir for less level, project across all rows, and as you move from one side to the other, the far speaker gradually takes over to keep the sound relatively even all the way across.

When there wasn't a convenient place to mount the monitors, I simply used 1-inch plumbing pipe with the screw-on flange at one end. The monitor is bolted to the flange, and the pipes are mounted to a rail with conduit brackets (or even inserted in a floor recess) and painted to match the decor. As you can see from the picture, this position can also cover an orchestra in front of the choir. The monitors can also be rotated in case you ever need some extra side fill monitoring on the front stage area for a special program.

Stereo Tracks

Churches have often used stereo cassette or CD soundtracks for singers and choirs. Hopefully, cassettes are a thing of the past, because you could get high-frequency phase cancellation between the left and right tracks through mono systems. This is the result of the tape being a mechanical format (unlike digital CD) and not aligning perfectly on the playback heads of various decks. The only ways around it are to use only one side of the cassette output (preferably the left to accommodate the music side of "split tracks") or to run the channel of the right side lower than the left to minimize phasing effects. Thankfully, with CDs, DVDs, and MP3 playback forcing out tape tracks, you won't have the phasing problem, since these are read digitally, not mechanically.

You can develop some "conducting" capabilities for music tracks as if you were leading an orchestra. Make sure soft beginnings are raised enough for the singers to get their cues. If dynamics seem to be lacking, you can drop back music slightly during verses and gradually swell the music while the last note is being held. You'd be surprised at the extra impact such subtle changes will add to a performance and an otherwise "flat" background. If necessary, consult with your music director on these techniques.

Feedback Control

Choir and lapel mics cause some of the greatest feedback difficulties, and they're good reason to insist on a mixer with at least one sweep frequency in the channel EQ. Without it, you can't address specific problem areas for individual mics. The first step is finding and controlling the few major feedback points, thereby smoothing out most of the rough spots. Afterward, you just have to be mindful that you have some limit to any given mic's level before feedback will start. Assuming you have at least 3-band, sweep mid EQ . . .

Gradually bring up a problem channel until slight, controlled feedback starts. If the feedback tone is a very low or very high frequency, cut back the appropriate Low or Hi fixed EQ knob a notch or two (3dB for each notch). If the tone sounds more in the middle ranges, turn the mid-frequency sweep knob all the way to the right, set the mid gain control at 10:00, and then rotate the frequency knob to the left until you hear the feedback dip or stop. Set the sweep at that point, then bring up the fader more to find and work out the next feedback point. If it's the previous one again, drop the appropriate EQ gain one more notch. If it's another mid-frequency close to the first, you may be able to compromise the sweep frequency position to catch them both. Test for a third feedback point unless you start getting two or three at once. Then stop. To go further will get you to a point of diminishing returns. Finish up by making subtle EQ adjustments for voice quality if necessary.

With a well-tuned system, I almost always have to roll back somewhere between 400Hz to 600Hz, as well as some low end on choir mics and omni lapels. (For the latter, try between 500Hz and 630Hz first.) The miniature podium condensers may require some similar adjustments. Good handheld mics don't give me any trouble, but acoustic piano mics may, depending on the level needed from them. Watch your stage monitor levels, too. If there is a consistent problem frequency here, take it down slightly on the monitor graphic EQ. If you have trouble locating feedback, a real-time analyzer will help. The answers will light up before your very eyes, and before long, you'll be able to approximate frequencies by ear.

I have a method for setting level on the most finicky mics to make it easy for the sound team to avoid feedback during the service—from the system and the pastor himself. After equalizing a lapel or podium mic, I'll bring down the input gain, set the channel fader at the unity gain "0" position, bring up the input gain until feedback starts, then back off a notch or so. I'll also set choir mics this way with all their faders up to account for the collective level. Once finished, I know that "0" is the highest I can safely go on the fader(s); any higher will be shaky ground. And we all know shaky ground and the solid rock don't mix.

Phase Reverse

There may come a time when a pastor with an active wireless lapel walks up to an active podium mic, and his voice suddenly becomes very thin or hollow-sounding. This is an indication that the mics are out of phase with each other for some reason. If you have phase reverse on your mixer, you can switch it on the podium mic. If not, reverse the hot and neutral wires on one XLR end of the podium mic cable. (This is easier than messing with the wireless system.) Also, due to phasing effects that can occur from varying distances between two mics even when they are in phase, it would be best to commit to one mic or the other instead of leaving them both on. Wireless wins if the pastor moves around.

Another timing problem can be caused by the combination of a pastor's voice projecting directly to a podium mic, and also bouncing into the mic off a hard podium surface. If you notice a problem, try some carpeting on the podium surface to absorb reflections. You may be able to get away with light gray or white on a clear Plexiglas podium. Clear carpet is very expensive and hard to come by.

Conservative Engineering

The catchword for conservative engineering in modest rooms is *sound reinforcement*, not replacement. Think about how close you can stay to natural sound levels rather than how much you can overpower them. In smaller churches, you'll be able to hear at least some remnant of the pastor's or performers' voices carry acoustically in the room. It just wouldn't be enough to distinguish everything clearly and get over music or background noise. So add just the level needed to accomplish that. Then sound retains a more natural quality. As with miking, trust your ear. If you can't hear what's being said, others won't be able to either. If it's loud to you, it's probably blasting Grandma in the front row. Use common sense for the common good.

A service can include spontaneous activity from pastors, music leaders, or members of the congregation as they are felt led. Don't be a robot, and be aware of what is going on and prepared to bring up speaking or wireless mics as needed. Most pastors have certain moves they make that indicate they're about to speak, so try to second-guess them. Don't wait until after they start before you bring them up, and don't use channel on/off switches for them. Use the faders for more gradual changes in case you miss a cue. In fact, I prefer to leave a pastor's wireless preset and let them cut their transmitter on and off as they choose. This takes the heat off us, but ultimately it's the pastor's choice. They have enough to think about without adapting to our whims.

Concentrate on the main music leader and instrument, normally piano or acoustic guitar, in the monitors. These will provide the primary vocal, pitch, and rhythm reference for all concerned. Be careful about feeding choir, lapel, or podium mics through nearby monitors since they're more prone to feedback. And as I mentioned in Chapter 2, if you need more choir level in the mains to get over full band and/or orchestra, try inconspicuous miking of eight to ten primary choir singers with wireless mini-headmics. A little expense, but it works great!

Another note about vocal mics. Some people think that you need to have mics meticulously tuned for each person. This is more of a subjective preference, but it is not absolutely necessary in a normal worship environment, with background vocalists changing every week and/or engineers who may be a bit weak on EQ technique. If you have matching mics tuned with equal fidelity and clarity, you will reproduce each vocal the way it sounds naturally. Unless someone has a really bad vocal tone, why would you try to make everyone sound identical? Just like an a cappella vocal group singing *au naturel*, their unique differences can actually enhance the density and separation of vocal parts. The moral: Keep it simple, and tune all your BGV mics the same; there will be less room for error, and the mics will work for any singers you put on them.

Hearing Assistance

Like wireless in-ear monitors, hearing-assistance systems by companies like Telex, Williams, Sennheiser, and Galaxy offer economical wireless transmission for the hard-of-hearing in churches and other public venues. This is actually required in public facilities by the American Disabilities Act (ADA). Since a common signal from the mixer will suffice for all these listeners, you can have a single transmitter and any number of wireless receivers on the same frequency to pass out to those who need them. The feed is best from a dedicated aux send used for a balanced recording mix, but you can use an aux or matrix to feed primarily voices, since lyrics, dialogue, and sermons are the priority.

Sometimes a policy that's easier on church funds is for users to buy and bring their own personal receivers (about $100 each, specific to the system used) or, for hygiene reasons, at least bring their own earbuds to use with the church's receivers. You can also use receivers in the nursery (if the system will transmit that far) so you won't need a remote speaker system that might wake the babies. Listening options include single and dual earbuds or induction loops that will transmit the receiver signal into hearing aids.

These systems can also be useful for some alternative purposes if you use your imagination. Most transmitters will accept a mic input as well, so I've used them to transmit foreign-language translations to non-English-speaking members of a congregation. Simply put the translator on headphones or in a position to hear the pastor, give him the mic connected to an HA transmitter, and pass out the receivers to whoever needs them.

While most HA systems have been low-band FM or VHF frequencies, the Galaxy AnySpot system has brought high-band UHF down to the same price range (about $1,000 for a package of transmitter + four

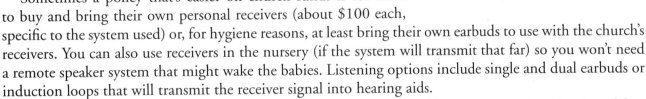

receivers) and is designed to serve as a wireless IEM as well. There are also some IR (infrared) systems with the purpose of avoiding potential wireless interference. These are meant for small rooms and, unlike RF systems, must be positioned to provide direct line-of-sight between the IR sensors of the transmitter and any receivers. They appear to be more popular and economical for small classroom use in schools and other educational facilities.

Service Recording

Some mixers indicate "dedicated" outputs for recording, but they are simply paralleled off the main outputs and probably won't give you a worthy mix unless it is sermon alone. Normally, you should use a post-fader aux send for easy individual channel control to balance the recording. If you don't have an aux send available and you're running a basic mono system off a stereo mixer, a convenient way to use pans again for an easy and individual recording feed is to use the Left output for Live sound and the Right for Recording. ("L" and "R." How convenient.) Start with all the channel pans centered. If certain channels are too loud on tape, pan them sufficiently to the left, reducing their level through the right output. Then bring up the overall on the recorder so that the overall level is good. If you use dedicated ambient mics to record the congregation, you can pan them full right so they only go to the recording.

Once these compensated recording "pan-levels" are set, normal operation for the house will balance properly on the recording. Any such recording feeds, whether this *pan* method or *aux sends*, are also useful for video capture, broadcast, and hearing-assistance systems, as well as peripheral speakers in the foyer, halls, nursery, etc.

CD and audio software recording has really helped ministries transition away from poor-quality cassettes. Sophisticated CD duplicators have replaced the slow and high-maintenance tape models, blank CDRs have become much cheaper than the lowest-grade cassette tape, there are flexible on-CD printing options, and audio can be transferred easily to computer for archiving, editing, and web access.

(Note: Be aware of laws about duplicating copyrighted music in church programs. Contact licensing organizations like CCLI about restrictions and clearances.)

Following are some final notes:

- Choose a mixer with phantom power and at least one sweep EQ on channels.
- Always buy low-impedance mics. (These use XLR, not 1/4-inch phone plugs.)
- For safety, consider mounting a wireless mic in the baptismal when needed. Wired mics, especially phantom-powered, can be an electrocution hazard.
- Don't buy speakers with *piezo* horns. Make sure they are *compression driver* horns.
- Always make sure elevated speakers are properly suspended and equipped with safety-approved standmount or hanging hardware.
- Always commend the worship leader on how lovely he or she looks today.

THEATRICAL SOUND

Theatre is very similar to church in that natural sound quality is a priority, especially with all the speaking parts involved. Due emphasis should be given to the natural blend of ambient and reinforced sound. But I also address this application specifically because of the potential number of wireless mics employed and the problems of amplifying all the dialogue or singing with so many mics. Unfortunately, the distance and movement of actors onstage usually renders fixed-mic pickup ineffective. Sometimes an upstage, floor-mounted, unidirectional boundary mic, like the Crown PCC-160, or a hanging choir mic can work for picking up individuals within an 8-foot square, or group speaking or singing within 15 feet if the system is tuned well and the actors can project and e-n-u-n-c-i-a-t-e. Otherwise, wireless lapel or mini-headmics are going to be your best bet.

For most situations, including churches and schools, $300 to $600 UHF wireless mics by companies like Audio-Technica, Sennheiser, and Shure do very well. You'll always need to be careful of damage to transmitter parts and cable connections, and you should keep receivers elevated and within 75 feet of the stage to avoid dropouts. Arrange workable mic passes to other actors if you're short a few systems. You could also purchase extra mics that can be precisely placed on performers ahead of time, and just exchange transmitters for quicker mic passes.

Lapel mics are often worn on the chest, but they can also be hidden in the hair with a barrette or placed over the ear and secured with clear surgical tape. In the absence of sinus problems, nostril placement offers excellent pickup if you can successfully hide the cable. (Now truthfully, how many of you actually considered this for a second?) I have also been able to spray-paint mics and cables to match hair, flesh, or clothing colors, but be sure to cover the cable connectors and the holes for the mic element while doing so.

Though considerably higher in cost than lapels, a better option is the "near invisible" mini-headmics, which come in a few different colors to blend with skin tones or beards. These omnidirectionals offer better level with less feedback if you don't mind them being slightly visible from the front rows. For stability, you can secure their behind-the-ear cables with clear surgical tape. Make sure the mic follows close to the cheek line to be as inconspicuous as possible and low enough to avoid breath pops. You don't want omnidirectionals in front of the mouth or even at the corners, where pops can occur. No windscreen is needed for this side placement, so the mic will be as small and invisible as possible.

With the physical nature of some dramatic productions, be ready for potential problems caused by perspiration getting into mic connections. To remedy this, place the mic in a dry area or seal vulnerable cable connectors with clear silicone sealer. Another preventive measure is to tape over transmitter on/off switches (if they don't have a cover or locking feature) so they don't accidentally get switched off during a performance. Leave active indicators visible if possible, and use gaffer's tape (not masking or duct tape) to avoid sticky glue buildup on the transmitter.

When engineering for the theatre, you've got to stay on top of the dialogue and make script notations accordingly. For my script cues, I notate mic numbers in the margins by the names when mic passes are involved. Then I don't have to label the mixer for every name that might be used. In a particular scene, I'll have all the appropriate mics up to moderate speaking levels and ride them up and down if needed as lines are spoken. Be sure to notate loud passages like yells, screams, whistles, etc. for a quick adjustment to avoid a few migraines in the audience. Digital mixers offer the distinct advantages of compressors on every channel to control levels, and memory recall to make sure numerous mics in a particular scene are all up and ready at the touch of a button.

You'll also notice that actors can be picked up through each other's mics if they are close to one another. To minimize the resulting effects, either ride their mics up and down according to their lines or, if they are real close or hugging, commit to one mic if you can get good pickup of both. As you become familiar with the parts and dialogue, you can actually get into a rhythm just as the actors do. And if there are prerecorded music and sound effects cues, have someone else control them to keep you focused on the wireless. It takes good script notes and some practice, but it's a rewarding feeling when the spontaneous spirit of engineering and dramatic performance come together as one soul-stirring entity.

SO, DO I HAVE TO PAINT YOU A PICTURE?

I guess you thought I'd forget! Yes, I understand how difficult it can be to put the whole thing together without a chart. I, too, have tried putting together Christmas toys! (Take my word for it: Audio is easier.) So as a final touch, I've included a graphic diagram of a complete sound system on the next page, with the major components, their page locations, and indications of connections and signal flow. I illustrate it from an analog perspective since a lot of these components will be hidden within digital mixers and processors, but "virtual" connection and configuration will follow the same guidelines. Diagrams such as this are provided in many equipment manuals (and should be), so refer to them for more specific information and various applications.

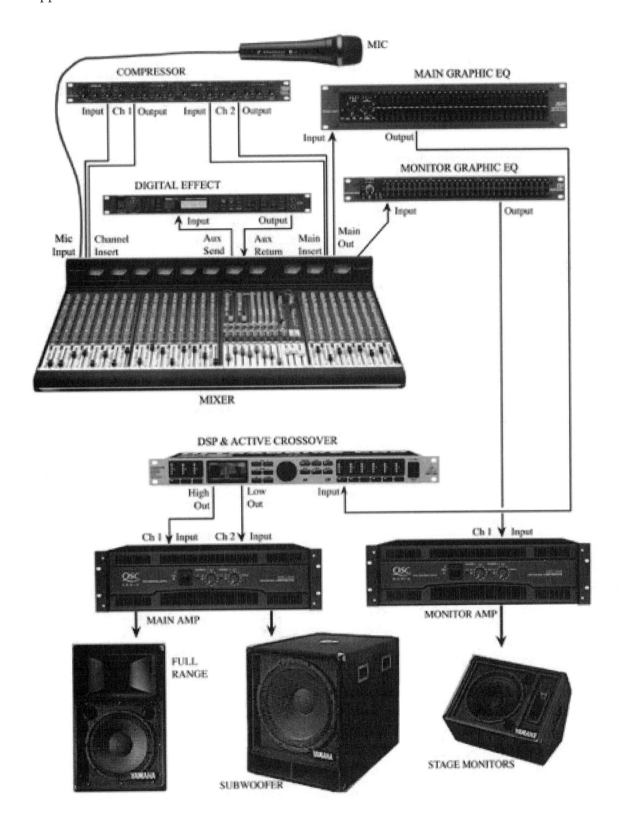

Packing Up

I THINK I'VE COVERED ABOUT EVERYTHING I WANTED TO, and quite frankly, I've run out of vocabulary. I pretty much stuck to what was in my head (as opposed to other areas), and I can't begin to remember where it all came from. A lot of trial and error and a few major screw-ups for sure. And it surprised me almost as much as my wife that this much stuff was actually in my brain! (Then she wonders why I can't remember to take out the trash. Data banks full, I explain.)

There are lots of good books that specialize in various areas of audio, and I encourage you to pursue them as your desire dictates. I only hope I've provided you with an abundance of valuable information here. If not, I probably won't retire with lots of book revenue, so I'll settle for what's left of Social Security and fast-food senior discounts.

Good luck to you, too. I trust you'll enjoy the same satisfaction and rewards that I have in this exciting, challenging, and ever-changing world of pro audio. Take your time, and thank you for giving me some of it.

"There's no business like show business, like no business I know . . ."

P.S. I wouldn't want to disappoint those of you who thought this section was about packing up equipment: "Don't scratch anything, and put the heavy stuff up front."

For those of you who wish to contact me with questions, comments, or critique (be gentle) . . .
Email: irawhiteaudio@gmail.com

ABOUT THE AUTHOR

IRA WHITE HAS BEEN INVOLVED IN THE MUSIC BUSINESS since 1971. Born in Norfolk, Virginia, he played professionally as a guitarist/singer for 15 years in various touring bands. He put together his first 8-track personal studio in 1983, which eventually expanded into a 16-track production facility. Work in retail music sales as well as live recording and engineering were a progressive outgrowth of his interests and contacts.

In 1992, he started Studio Street in Virginia Beach, a pro audio store and consulting/installation firm, which evolved into Sanctuary Sound, Inc., to focus on ministry needs and training. He also worked as a sound director for local ministries, served as a worship leader, and is still involved in independent recording and engineering. Other sound projects have included TMCJ International Productions and worship artist Paul Wilbur's Lion of Judah tour in the U.S. and Costa Rica.

In 2008, Ira became tech director for Deep Creek Baptist Church in Chesapeake, Virginia. He resides in nearby Portsmouth with his wife, Susan. His hobbies are scuba diving, video editing, traveling, and discussing audio with his dog Mercy, who has excellent high-frequency perception. Ira can be contacted at irawhiteaudio@gmail.com.

INDEX